Treasure Chest

Practice Book

GRADE 2

D1408263

Macmillan/McGraw-Hill

How to Use this Book

Based on the needs of your English Language Learners, you may need to accommodate how to use this book with your students.

- Read the directions with students and review any visuals or labels on the page.

- Work through the examples with students as a group, modeling how to fill in the pages.

- Have students work in pairs, pairing more proficient English speakers with less proficient English speakers.

At the bottom of each page, additional suggestions are provided including ways to address the English Language Learners at the Beginning/Intermediate levels.

B

 Macmillan/McGraw-Hill

Published by Macmillan/McGraw-Hill, of McGraw-Hill Education, a division of The McGraw-Hill Companies, Inc., Two Penn Plaza, New York, New York 10121.

Printed in the United States of America

4 5 6 7 8 9 HES 14 13 12 11

Contents

Unit 4 • Better Together

Unit 5 • Growing and Changing

Unit 6 • The World Around Us

Name _____

Listen to your teacher read *School Star* aloud. Use the Character and Setting Chart below to take notes. Then retell the story.

Character	Setting

Beginning/Intermediate Read the directions. Remind children to identify important people and think about the time and place of the story events as they listen to the story. Explain to children how and where they should take notes on the chart.

Name _____

Phonics/Word Study: Short *a, i*

Circle the word with the short *a* sound.

1.

cat

cow

2.

bowl

bag

Circle the word with the short *i* sound. Say the word.

3.

pig

pan

4.

ring

cat

© Macmillan/McGraw-Hill

Beginning/Intermediate Review how to decode. Point to and name the pictures. Point out your mouth position. Have children repeat and practice saying the words with a partner. Have them listen to the **Sound Pronunciation CD**.

Phonics: Consonant Blends

Circle the consonant blend *sl*, *sp*, *sk*, or *st* in each word.

1.

nest

2.

skating

3.

spoon

4.

slide

Circle the word with the consonant blend. Then write the word on the line. Say the word.

5. slip   kite   hit   *Kite hit*

6. bee   stem   eat   *Bee eat*

7. skate   bat   bean   *Bat Bean*

Read the Decodable Reader *Pat and Tim* with a partner. Look at page 6 of the story. Point to the signs on the door.

Beginning/Intermediate Read and point to examples 1–4. Have partners complete all the examples and say words 5–7 to each other. Tell children they may often see print in the world around them. They may see street signs, shop names, and posters. Point to the signs on page 6 of the Decodable Reader. Read the environmental print aloud and have children repeat.

Use the word chart to study this week's vocabulary words. Write a sentence using each word in your writer's notebook.

Word	Context Sentence	Illustration
groan I groan when my fabrit tox fell an brok	Sam let out a <u>groan</u> when he spilled his milk.	
excited _____	I like school and am <u>excited</u> to be here.	 **Describe how you feel when you are excited.**
whisper _____	I <u>whisper</u> a secret to my friend.	
carefully _____	I gave him the glass <u>carefully</u> so the juice would not spill.	 **What do you do carefully?**
different _____	I am wearing two <u>different</u> shoes!	

© Macmillan/McGraw-Hill

Beginning/Intermediate Review vocabulary. Use gestures to demonstrate meaning. Pair children to write one or two sentences, or draw pictures, to illustrate the meaning of the newly acquired vocabulary.

Name _____

Grammar: Statements and Questions
**Read the sentences below. Circle each question.
Underline each statement.**

1. The rain comes down.

2. Who will go out in the rain?

3. Ann will go out.

4. What will Ann do in the rain?

**Read the sentences. Circle the sentence that is
written correctly.**

5. Ann plays in the puddles.

   Ann plays in the puddles

6. does she like to splash

   Does she like to splash?

7. Can Ann stay dry?

   can Ann stay dry

8. no, Ann will get wet

   No, Ann will get wet.

Beginning/Intermediate Read the directions for each section and
model the first example. Have children work with partners to complete
examples and say sentences to each other.

Write About It

Use story details to support your answers. Use the lines below or another sheet of paper.

1. What problem does Tim have at the beginning of the story?

   _____

   _____

2. What does Tim decide to do when he sees the poster?

   _____

   _____

Remember to:

- Take turns speaking and listening.

- Ask and answer questions about the story.

- Use the new words you have learned.

- Use your own experiences to help you understand.

Talk About It

Discuss your answers to questions 1–2 and the questions below with a partner or group.

3. Tell about something you are good at doing.

4. Are you and Tim good at the same things or different things?

5 What do you predict Tim will do at the next soccer game?

Beginning/Intermediate Read the directions and questions aloud. Have children express their ideas and opinions to the group. Guide them to use academic language in their responses. You may wish to have children listen to the selection on the **Audio CD**.

Listen to your teacher read *City Garden* aloud. Use the Plot Chart below to take notes. Then retell the story.

Beginning

Middle

End

Beginning/Intermediate Read the directions. Remind children to look for key visual details and think about events as they listen to the story. Explain to children how and where they should take notes on the chart.

Grade 2 Unit I Week 2   7

Name _____

Phonics/Word Study: Short *e, o, u*
Circle the word that names each picture.

1.    (shell)   ship

2.    sand   (sun)

3.    man   (mop)

Fill in the blank to complete each word. Say the word.

4.    l _____ g

5.    f _____ x

6.    p _____ p

Beginning/Intermediate Review how to decode. Point to and name the pictures. Point out your mouth position. Have children repeat and practice saying the words with a partner. Have them listen to the **Sound Pronunciation CD**.

© Macmillan/McGraw-Hill

Name _____

Phonics: Consonant Digraphs

Circle the word with the consonant digraph *ch* or *th* in each row. Then write the word on the line. Say the word.

1.	three	tag	ten	*three*
2.	can	cat	cheer	*cheer*
3.	top	ton	thank	*thand*
4.	luck	lunch	lot	*lunch*
5.	chip	can	cap	*chip*
6.	want	with	wing	*want*

Sight Words

Circle the word you hear. Write the word.

7.	the	to	said	*to*
8.	some	can	little	*can*
9.	you	was	are	*you*
10.	do	they	of	*of*

Read the Decodable Reader *Len and Gus* with a partner. Find the words *do, are, said, some*.

Beginning/Intermediate 1–6: Model example 1 and say the words for children to repeat. 7–10: Say the sight word in each row (said, some, are, do). Ask children to repeat the word you say before they circle and write the word.

Grade 2 Unit 1 Week 2 9

Name _____

**Use the word chart to study this week's vocabulary words.
Write a sentence using each word in your writer's notebook.**

Word	Context Sentence	Illustration
share _____	We can <u>share</u> the ice cream.	
enjoyed _____	We <u>enjoyed</u> the ice cream.	
wonderful _____	The ice cream tastes <u>wonderful</u>.	**What food tastes wonderful to you?**
thinning _____	The crowd is <u>thinning</u> out as people leave the game.	
delighted _____	I am <u>delighted</u> to see you!	
company _____	My cat keeps me <u>company</u> at night.	

© Macmillan/McGraw-Hill

Beginning/Intermediate Review vocabulary. Use gestures to demonstrate meaning. Pair children to write sentences, or draw pictures, to illustrate the meaning of the newly acquired vocabulary and tell sentences to each other.

Grammar: Commands and Exclamations

Read each sentence aloud to a partner. Circle the word that tells if the sentence is an exclamation or a command.

1. You scored a goal!

   command   (exclamation)

2. Pass me a pencil.

   (command)   exclamation

3. Do not go to bed late.

   (command)   exclamation

4. We had a great day!

   command   (exclamation)

Write an exclamation point (!) on the line if the sentence is an exclamation. Write a period (.) if the sentence is a command.

5. We won _____

6. Get the ball _____

7. Please share your toys _____

Beginning/Intermediate Read the directions for each section and model the first example. Point out the exclamation point. Have children work with partners to complete examples and say sentences to each other.

Grade 2 Unit 1 Week 2   11

© Macmillan/McGraw-Hill

Write About It

Use story details to support your answers. Use the lines below or another sheet of paper.

1. What does Matt want to do at the beginning of the story? Write a sentence.

   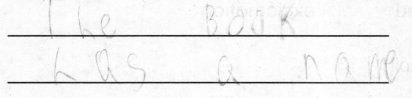

   The Book
   has a name

2. Write about something that happens in the middle of the story.

   _____

   _____

Remember to:

- Listen carefully to your classmates.

- Ask and answer questions about the story.

- Use the new words you have learned.

- Retell what you hear to check understanding.

Talk About It

Discuss your answers to questions 1–2 and the questions below with a partner or group.

3. What must Matt and Mrs. Choi do before they plant their garden?

4. Do people like the garden? How do you know?

5. What happens when people work together to do big jobs?

Beginning/Intermediate Read the directions and questions aloud. Guide children's written responses. Encourage children to use story details and their own experiences during the discussion. You may wish to have children listen to the selection on the **Audio CD**.

© Macmillan/McGraw-Hill

Listen to your teacher read *Family History* aloud. Use the Main Idea and Details Chart below to take notes. Then retell this book.

Detail	Detail	Detail

Main Idea

Beginning/Intermediate Read the directions. As children listen to the story, work together to identify important details in the text. Help children use the details to determine the main idea. Explain how and where they should take notes on the chart.

Name _____

Phonics/Word Study: Short *a* and Long *a* (*a – e*)
Circle the word with the short *a* sound.

1.
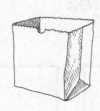
(bag)

book

2.
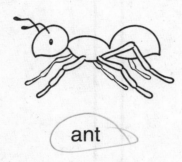
(ant)

bowl

3.

cow

cap

Circle the word with the long *a* sound.
Then write the word on the line. Say the word.

4. (cake)   cap   cup   _cake_

5. skin   (skate)   ship   _skate_

6. run   rod   (rake)   _rake_

7. sleep   (sack)   snake   _sake_

© Macmillan/McGraw-Hill

Beginning/Intermediate Review how to decode. Point to and name
the pictures. Point out your mouth position. Have children repeat and
practice saying the words with a partner. Have them listen to the **Sound
Pronunciation CD**.

Phonics: Consonant Blends *sl, dr, sk, sp, st*
Circle the word that completes each sentence. Write the word on the line. Then circle the consonant blend in the word.

1. Peg likes many _sports_.

   (sports)   slim

2. She likes to _skate_.

   drove   skate

3. She has fun on _skis_.

   (skis)   spoon

4. Today her family _drives_ to the hills.

   (drives)   down

Sight Words
Listen to each sentence that is read. Write the word that is missing.

done	another	put	they

5. Tim _put_ his sled in the car.

6. He is _done_ sledding.

7. His sister will pick _another_ sport.

8. _they_ will play.

Read the Decodable Reader *You Can Bake a Cake!* with a partner. Find the words *put, another, some, done.*

Beginning/Intermediate 1–4: Say the words for each sound. Have children repeat. Ask partners to read the sentences. 5–8: Ask children to repeat the completed sentence after you, before writing the missing word.

Grade 2 Unit 1 Week 3   15

Use the word chart to study this week's vocabulary words. Write a sentence using each word in your writer's notebook.

Word	Context Sentence	Illustration
harvest _____	The apples are red and ready to <u>harvest</u>.	
crops _____	Some farmers sell their <u>crops</u> at the market.	**What other crops might you find at the market?**
regrow _____	We <u>regrow</u> the same plants in our garden every year.	
machines _____	Some families have these <u>machines</u> in the basement.	**What are these machines used for?**
irrigate _____	Pipes bring water to <u>irrigate</u> the field.	

Beginning/Intermediate Review vocabulary. Use gestures to demonstrate meaning. Pair children to write sentences, or draw pictures, to illustrate the meaning of the newly acquired vocabulary and tell sentences to each other.

Name _____

Grammar: Subjects

Circle the subject in each sentence.

1. An alarm rings.

2. Firefighters jump into the fire truck.

3. You tell the person about the fire.

4. Smoke can hurt you.

5. People call 911 for help.

Look at the picture below. Write a sentence that tells what is happening in the picture. Then circle the subject in your sentence.

They are haveing a piknik

Beginning/Intermediate Read each set of directions and model the first example. Have partners circle the subjects and write sentences. Have children share their sentences with the group.

Grade 2 Unit 1 Week 3   17

Name _____

Write About It

Use story details to support your answers. Use the lines below or another sheet of paper.

1. What is an important idea in this book?

_____

_____

2. Write a sentence about a family in this book.

_____

_____

Remember to:

- Take turns speaking and listening.

- Ask and answer questions about the story.

- Use the new words you have learned.

- Share a personal experience.

Talk About It

Discuss your answers to questions 1–2 and the questions below with a partner or group.

3. What would you like to learn about your family's history?

4. What is a way that many families are alike?

Go to the Online Oral Language Activities and slideshow for Unit 1: Coming to America to hear more about family history. Share what you learned with a partner.

© Macmillan/McGraw-Hill

Beginning/Intermediate Read the directions and questions aloud. Guide children's written responses. Prompt children to use content-area vocabulary, such as *history* and *traditions*, in the discussion. You may wish to have children listen to the selection on the **Audio CD**.

Name_____

Listen to your teacher read *Three American Heroes* aloud. Use the Main Idea and Details Chart below to take notes. Then retell the book.

Beginning/Intermediate Read the directions. As children listen to the story and work together to determine the main idea. Ask children to identify details in the text that support the main idea. Explain how and where they should take notes on the chart.

Name_____

Phonics/Word Study: Long *i* (*i – e*) and Short *i*
Write the word that names the picture on the line.

1.

mouse

2.

Fire

3.

slid

4.

Bike

Underline the word with the short *i* sound. Say the word.

5.   fish   fun   fine

6.   pen   pin   pine

7.   door   do   dish

Beginning/Intermediate Review how to decode words. In each section, read and point to one word with the new sound. Point out your mouth position. Have children say the words. Children can listen to the **Sound Pronunciation CD**.

© Macmillan/McGraw-Hill

Name_____

Phonics: Soft *c* and *g*

got	guess	city	cell
gentle	face	car	gerbil
cent	germ	cage	good

Read each word in the box. Listen for soft c and soft g. Write the word in the correct box below.

Soft *c*	Soft *g*
1. cent	5. got
2. car	6. gentle
3. cage	7. good
4. cell	8. germ

Choose words from the soft c or soft g list to complete each sentence. Write the word on the line.

9. Ken has a big smile on his _____ FACe _____.

10. He just got a pet _____ cat _____.

11. He keeps his pet in a _____ cage _____.

12. His new pet is very _____ cute _____.

Read the Decodable Reader *Mike's Big Bike* with a partner.

Beginning/Intermediate Read each set of directions. Model examples I and 5. Say each word for children to repeat. Have partners complete the examples and say the words. Children can listen to the **Sound Pronunciation CD**.

Use the word chart to study this week's vocabulary words.

Write a sentence using each word in your writer's notebook.

Word	Context Sentence	Illustration
cultures _____	These people come from many <u>cultures</u>.	**What culture do you come from?**
deaf _____	She cannot hear because she is <u>deaf</u>.	
signing _____	She is <u>signing</u> the words "I love you."	
relatives _____	My aunt and other <u>relatives</u> came for dinner.	
celebrate _____	They came to <u>celebrate</u> my birthday.	**How do you celebrate a special time?**

Beginning/Intermediate/Advanced/Advanced High Review vocabulary. Use gestures to demonstrate meaning. Pair children to write sentences, or draw pictures, to illustrate the meaning of the newly acquired vocabulary and tell

Name_____

Grammar: Predicates
Underline the predicate of each sentence.

1. Guide dogs are special dogs.

2. Guide dogs help blind people.

3. The dogs go to guide dog school.

4. Guide dogs learn hand signals.

Write a sentence about the picture.
Then circle the predicate in your sentence.

5.

_____

6.

_____

Beginning/Intermediate Read the directions for each section and model the first example. Have children work with partners to complete examples. Have them share their sentences with the group.

Grade 2 Unit I Week 4   23

© Macmillan/McGraw-Hill

Book Talk

Write About It

Use story details to support your answers. Use the lines below or another sheet of paper.

1. What is a hero? Write a sentence.

   _____

   _____

2. What did Dr. Martin Luther King, Jr., want?

   _____

   _____

Remember to:

- Listen carefully to your classmates.

- Use what you already know to help you understand.

- Use the new words you have learned.

Talk About It

Discuss your answers to questions 1–2 and the questions below with a partner or group.

3. Tell why Jane Addams was a hero.

4. How are the three heroes in this book alike?

5. What are some ways you can be a hero in your own community?

You can use informal English when you talk to other students. Some phrases you may use are *What do you mean?, Like what?,* and *Yeah*.

© Macmillan/McGraw-Hill

Beginning/Intermediate Read the directions and questions aloud. Guide children's written responses. Help children make connections among ideas by pointing out similarities. Remind children they may use informal English with classmates.

Listen to your teacher read *Remember Me* aloud. Use the Predictions Chart below to take notes. Then retell this story.

What I Predict	What Happens

Beginning/Intermediate Read the directions. Guide children to see how chapter titles can help them predict story events. Explain to children how and where they should take notes on the chart as they listen to the story.

Grade 2 Unit I Week 5 25

Name _____

Phonics/Word Study: Short *o, u* and Long *o (o – e), u (u – e)*

Circle the word with the short *o* or short *u* sound.

1.

rope

knot

2.

goat

fox

3.

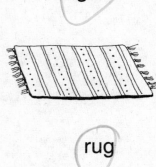

rug

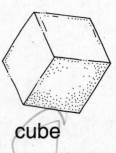

cube

**Circle the word with the long *o* or long *u* sound.
Then write the word on the line. Say the word.**

4. nose   nine   net   _____

5. sock   stone   sea   _____

6. mud   mat   mule   _____

7. cute   comb   cub   _____

Beginning/Intermediate Read and point to the words in examples 1–3 to give examples of the four new sounds. Point out your mouth position. Have children say the words with a partner. Children can listen to the **Sound Pronunciation CD.**

Name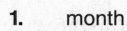_____

Phonics: Consonant Digraphs
Circle the word that names the picture.
Say the word.

1. month   meal

2. chore   chair

3. fish   fig

4. whales   watch

Circle each word with *tch, sh, th* or *ph*.
Write the word on the line.

5. wash   waste   _____

6. tree   both   _____

7. catch   cat   _____

8. graph   grab   _____

Read the Decodable Reader *At Home in Nome* with a partner.

Beginning/Intermediate Read and point to the words in examples 1–4.
Have partners repeat them to each other. Review word meaning.

Vocabulary

Use the word chart to study this week's vocabulary words.
Write a sentence using each word in your writer's notebook.

Word	Context Sentence	Illustration
patient _____	We are <u>patient</u> as we wait to slide.	
practiced _____	I <u>practiced</u> writing my name in English.	
favorite _____	Mom made my <u>favorite</u> meal.	**What is your favorite meal?**
wrinkled _____	My dog has a <u>wrinkled</u> face.	
settled _____	I am <u>settled</u> in a chair with a good book.	
cuddle _____	I like to <u>cuddle</u> my dog.	

Beginning/Intermediate Review vocabulary. Use gestures to demonstrate meaning. Pair children to write sentences, or draw pictures, to illustrate the meaning of the newly acquired vocabulary and tell sentences to each other.

Grammar: Sentence Combining

**Combine the sentences. Use *and* in the new sentence.
Say your sentences with a partner.**

1. Lions run. Tigers run.

_____

2. Billy sleeps. Billy wakes up.

_____

3. Julie has a bike. She has a book.

_____

**Look at the picture. Write one sentence about the girl
and one sentence about the boy. Then
combine the sentences.**

_____

_____

Beginning/Intermediate Read the directions for each section and
model the first example. Have children work with partners to write their
sentences. Have them share their sentences with the group.

Grade 2 Unit 1 Week 5 29

Write About It

Use story details and vocabulary to support your answers. Use the lines below or another sheet of paper.

1. What is difficult about Remember's new life? Write one sentence.

   _____

   _____

2. What does Remember learn from her new friend Sanu?

   _____

   _____

Remember to:

- Take turns speaking and listening.

- Share a personal experience.

- Use the new words you have learned.

- Ask for help when you don't understand.

Talk About It

Discuss your answers to questions 1–2 and the questions below with a partner or group.

3. Would you like to live on a ship? Tell why or why not.

4. What do you predict Remember will say about the big feast?

5. What are some ways you can show you are thankful?

© Macmillan/McGraw-Hill

Beginning/Intermediate Read the directions and questions aloud. Guide children's written responses. Help children make connections between the story and their own experiences. Prompt them to use academic language during the discussion.

Name_____

Listen to your teacher read *Ice Cool* aloud. Use the Character, Setting, Plot Chart below to take notes. Then retell the story.

Character

↓

Setting

↓

Beginning

↓

Middle

↓

End

© Macmillan/McGraw-Hill

Beginning/Intermediate Read the directions. Remind children to look for key visual details and think about events as they listen to the story. Have them narrate portions of the story to a partner. Explain to children how and where they should take notes on the chart.

Grade 2 Unit 2 Week I   31

Phonics/Word Study: Long *a*
Circle the word with the long *a* sound.

1.

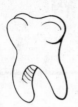

       tooth   train

2.

       rain   read

3.

       pen   pear

4.

       nail   nest

Circle the word with the long *a* sound.
Then write the word on the line. Say the word.

5. corn   tail   then   _____

6. play   pat   sun   _____

Beginning/Intermediate Review how to decode words. Read and point to two words with the long *a* sound (*train, rain*). Point out your mouth position. Have children say the words with a partner. Children can listen to the **Sound Pronunciation CD**.

Name _____

Phonics: Consonant Blends
Circle the word that names the picture.

1.   stain   step   strawberry

2.   scrap   short   speak

3.   play   stay   spray

4.   strong   song   speak

Circle each word with *scr, spr,* or *str*. Then write the word on the line. Say the word.

5.   strike   sock   _____

6.   beach   spread   _____

7.   spring   sing   _____

8.   alone   scrape   _____

Read the Decodable Reader *Watch the Birch Tree* with a partner.

© Macmillan/McGraw-Hill

Beginning/Intermediate Read and point to examples 1–4. Have partners complete all the examples and say words 5–8 to each other.

Grade 2 Unit 2 Week I   33

**Use the word chart to study this week's vocabulary words.
Write a sentence using each word in your writer's notebook.**

Word	Context Sentence	Illustration
exclaimed _____	"She scored another goal!" Dad <u>exclaimed</u>.	
concern _____	My mother's <u>concern</u> was that I broke my leg.	**When might you have concern for someone?**
vendors _____	The food <u>vendors</u> sold hot dogs, ice cream, and popcorn.	
figure _____	The prize was a <u>figure</u> of a soccer player scoring a goal.	
collection _____	My brother has a <u>collection</u> of stamps from all over the world.	**What kind of a collection would you rather have —stamps or shells?**

© Macmillan/McGraw-Hill

Beginning/Intermediate Review vocabulary. Use gestures to demonstrate meaning. Pair children to write sentences, or draw pictures, to illustrate the meaning of the newly acquired vocabulary and tell sentences to each other.

Name _____

Grammar: Nouns
Circle all the nouns in each sentence.

1. Julia eats salad for dinner.

2. The children are playing with the ball.

3. Raj rides his bike every day.

4. Trees have leaves and roots.

Write a sentence about the picture. Circle each noun in your sentence.

_____

_____

Beginning/Intermediate Read the directions for each section and model the first example. Have children work with partners to circle the nouns and write a sentence. Have them share their sentence with the group.

Write About It

Use story details to support your answers. Use the lines below or another sheet of paper.

1. Write a sentence that tells how Karl learned to skate.

   _____

   _____

2. What do you need to play hockey?

   _____

   _____

Remember to:

- Ask about words you don't know.

- Listen carefully to classmates.

- Use gestures to help show what you mean.

- Choose the right words.

Talk About It

Discuss your answers to questions 1–2 and the questions with a partner or group.

3. Is it cold where Karl's grandmother lives? How do you know?

4. What would you save for someone else to use? Why?

5. What new game have you learned to play? Tell one thing you like about the game.

Use the new words you have learned. Ask your partner and your teacher to help you tell about the story.

Beginning/Intermediate Read the directions and questions aloud. Guide children's written responses. Monitor and support children's efforts to pronounce new words correctly. Encourage partners to help one another infer meaning from the illustrations.

Listen to the story. Use the Cause and Effect Chart below to take notes. Work with your partner to retell the information in this book.

Cause → Effect

Beginning/Intermediate Read the directions. Remind children to look for key visual details and story events as they listen. Discuss the implicit reasons that some story events took place. Explain to children how and where they should take notes on the chart.

Grade 2 Unit 2 Week 2   37

Phonics/Word Study: Long *e*
Circle the word with the long e sound.
Say the word.

1.   seal   sing

2.   bed   bee

3.   tree   ten

Circle the word with the long e sound.
Write the word on the line.

4. chase   chief   _____

5. eat   full   _____

6. laugh   baby   _____

Beginning/Intermediate Review how to decode words. Read and point to two words with the long *e* sound (*seal, bee*). Point out your mouth position. Have children say the words and listen to the **Sound Pronunciation CD**.

Phonics: Prefixes *re-, un-, dis-*
Underline the words that have prefixes. Then write the words.

1. Pam seems unable to start her day.

   _____

2. Her hair is uncombed.

   _____

3. Her mother is displeased.

   _____

   _____

5. Pam disappears into her room.

   _____

6. Then she reappears in new clothes.

   _____

7. "Now I will redo everything," says Pam.

   _____

8. Pam will replace a bad day with a good one.

   _____

Read the Decodable Reader *It Won't Be Easy!* with a partner.

Beginning/Intermediate For each prefix, say one word for children to repeat. Read the directions and model the first example.

Grade 2 Unit 2 Week 2 39

Use the word chart to study this week's vocabulary words. Write a sentence using each word in your writer's notebook.

Word	Context Sentence	Illustration
advice _____	The coach gave me good <u>advice</u>.	**Who else might give you advice?**
commotion _____	Our dog makes a <u>commotion</u> when the phone rings.	
rattled _____	The branches <u>rattled</u> against the window when the wind blew.	
respected _____	Everyone <u>respected</u> the famous scientist.	**Name someone you respect. Why?**
shivering _____	I was <u>shivering</u> in my thin jacket.	
tangle _____	The kittens turned the balls of yarn into a messy <u>tangle</u>.	

© Macmillan/McGraw-Hill

Beginning/Intermediate Review vocabulary. Use gestures to demonstrate meaning. Pair children to write sentences, or draw pictures, to illustrate the meaning of the newly acquired vocabulary and tell sentences to each other.

Name _____

Grammar: Plural Nouns

Circle the words that name more than one.

1. brushes   boy   baby

2. books   pages   family

3. kittens   puppy   mess

Write a plural noun for each picture.

4.

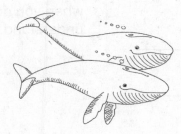

_____

5.

_____

6.

_____

7.

_____

Beginning/Intermediate Read the directions for each section and model examples 1 and 4. Have children work with partners to complete the examples. Have them say the plural nouns to each other.

© Macmillan/McGraw-Hill

Grade 2 Unit 2 Week 2   41

Write About It

Use story details to support your answers. Use the lines below or another sheet of paper.

1. What did cowboys long ago use to round up cattle?

_____

_____

2. What do cowboys today use to round up cattle?

_____

_____

Remember to:

- Listen to the speaker.

- Retell what you hear.

- Use the new words you have learned.

- Ask for help when you don't understand.

Talk About It

Discuss your answers to questions 1–2 and the questions below with a partner or group.

3. Cowboys long ago worked hard. What made their work dangerous?

4. What is the Goodnight-Loving Trail?

5. Think about a cowboy's work. Would you like to be a cowboy? Why or why not?

© Macmillan/McGraw-Hill

Beginning/Intermediate Read the directions and questions aloud. Guide children's written responses. During the discussion, encourage children to elaborate on their answers. You may wish to have children listen to the selection on the **Audio CD.**

Listen to your teacher read *Wildfires* aloud. Use the Main Idea and Details Chart below to take notes. Then retell what you learned.

Detail	Detail	Detail

Main Idea

Beginning/Intermediate Read the directions. As children listen to the story, work together to identify important details in the text. Help children use the details to determine the main idea. Explain how and where they should take notes on the chart.

Grade 2 Unit 2 Week 3 43

Name_____

Phonics/Word Study: Long *i*

Circle the word with the long *i* sound.

1.

cry   cup

2.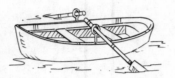

boat   sky

3.

pie   dish

4.

night   nail

Circle the word with the long *i* sound.
Then write the word on the line. Say the word.

5.   tie   the   _____

6.   lamp   light   _____

7.   fight   new   _____

Beginning/Intermediate Review how to decode words. Read and point to two words with the long *i* sound (*cry, sky*). Point out your mouth position. Have children say the words. Children can listen to the **Sound Pronunciation CD**.

© Macmillan/McGraw-Hill

Name _____

Phonics: Compound Words

Add the two words in each row to make a compound word. Say the word.

1. snow   +   storm   =   _____

2. chalk   +   board   =   _____

3. play   +   ground   =   _____

4. dog   +   house   =   _____

5. grass   +   lands   =   _____

**Write a word from the box to make a compound word.
Write the new word on the line.**

bed	week	fast

6. _____ + end   =   _____

7. _____ + room   =   _____

8. break + _____   =   _____

Read the Decodable Reader *Franny's Rain Forest* with a partner.

© Macmillan/McGraw-Hill

Beginning/Intermediate For each section, read the directions and
model the first example. Have partners say the words to each other.
Have children listen to the **Sound Pronunciation CD**.

**Use the word chart to study this week's vocabulary words.
Write a sentence using each word in your writer's notebook.**

Word	Context Sentence	Illustration
independence _____	My dad walks to school with me. Teenagers have the <u>independence</u> to walk to school alone.	How else do teenagers show their <u>independence</u>?
landmark _____	Visitors take a boat to see this <u>landmark</u>.	
state _____	Texas is the name of the <u>state</u> where we live.	**TEXAS** What is the name of another <u>state</u>?
government _____	The U.S. Capitol is an important <u>government</u> building.	
symbol _____	This <u>symbol</u> stands for "poison."	

© Macmillan/McGraw-Hill

Beginning/Intermediate Review vocabulary. Use gestures to demonstrate meaning. Pair children to write sentences, or draw pictures, to illustrate the meaning of the newly acquired vocabulary and tell sentences to each other.

Name _____

Grammar: Proper Nouns
Circle all the proper nouns.

1. My friend lives in Chicago.

2. Mr. Brown teaches at my school.

3. Doctor Hall helped Julie feel better.

4. Jim works at Riverdale Hospital.

Write your name and the name of your school on the lines.

_____

_____

© Macmillan/McGraw-Hill

Beginning/Intermediate Read the directions for each section and model the first example. Have partners complete examples 2–4. Have each child complete the bottom section and read their names to a partner.

Write About It

Use story details and vocabulary to support your answers. Use the lines below or another sheet of paper.

1. How can firefighters get water to a fire?

   _____

   _____

2. Why do firefighters sometimes start a small fire?

   _____

   _____

Remember to:

- Ask and answer questions about the story.

- Draw a picture to help show what you mean.

- Choose the right words.

- Use the new words you have learned.

Talk About It

Discuss your answers to questions 1–2 and the questions below with a partner or group.

3. What do you think firefighters see, smell, and feel when they fight a wildfire? Give details.

4. Explain why spacecraft are important when fighting a very large wildfire.

5. What one fact about wildfires do you want to share with a family member or friend?

© Macmillan/McGraw-Hill

Beginning/Intermediate Read the directions aloud. Guide children's written responses. Have children imagine they are firefighters and describe what they see and feel. Encourage them to use vocabulary words and details from the book as they role play fighting a wildfire.

Listen to your teacher read *Cinderella: A Tale From France* aloud. Use the Inference Chart below to take notes. Then retell the story.

What I Read	What I Know

Inference

Beginning/Intermediate Read the directions. Remind children to listen and look for key details and events as they listen to the story and make connections. Explain to children how and where they should take notes on the chart.

Grade 2 Unit 2 Week 4   49

Name _____

Phonics /Word Study: Long *o*

Circle the word that names the picture.
Then write the word on the line.

1. _____

   bowl   ball

2. _____

   coach   cot

3. _____

   dot   doe

Underline the word with the long *o* sound. Say the word.

4.   soap   sun   sand

5.   three   toe   that

6.   get   got   goat

7.   take   throw   took

Beginning/Intermediate Review how to decode words. Read and point to the first three words with the long o sound. Point out your mouth position. Have children say the words and listen to the **Sound Pronunciation CD**.

Name_____

Phonics: Inflectional Endings
**Circle the word that completes each sentence.
Write the word on the line.**

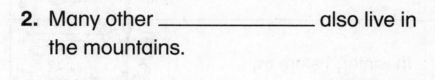

1. Yaks live high in the _____.

   mountains   mountain

2. Many other _____ also live in
   the mountains.

   animal   animals

3. Yaks are great _____.

   beast   beasts

4. They have a lot of fur and long _____.

   horns   horn

Write the new word on the line. Say the word.

5. field + s = _____

6. bus + es = _____

7. puddle + s = _____

8. law + s = _____

Read the Decodable Reader *Three Goats and a Troll* with a partner.

Beginning/Intermediate For each section, read the directions and
model one example. Point out that *buses* ends in *-es*. Have children
listen to the **Sound Pronunciation CD**.

Grade 2 Unit 2 Week 4   51

Use the word chart to study this week's vocabulary words.
Write a sentence using each word in your writer's notebook.

Word	Context Sentence	Illustration
collectors _____	The collectors looked at the stamps they had gathered.	
store _____	In winter, I store my bike in the shed.	
clever _____	My clever dog brings her leash when she wants to walk.	
reward _____	I reward my dog with a hug when she obeys a command.	**Why might someone be rewarded?**
double _____	John has double the homework of Max.	
amount _____	What amount do I owe you?	

Beginning/Intermediate Review vocabulary. Use gestures to demonstrate meaning. Pair children to write sentences, or draw pictures, to illustrate the meaning of the newly acquired vocabulary and tell sentences to each other.

Name _____

Grammar: Possessive Nouns
Circle the possessive nouns.

1. bird's   bats   trees

2. teachers   books   girl's

3. friends   mother's   houses

Write the possessive form of the noun in ( ) on the line. Say the sentence.

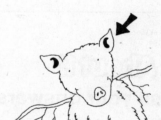

4. The _____ nest is in the tree.
   (bird)

5. The _____ ears are very big.
   (bat)

6. My _____ birthday is today.
   (friend)

7. The _____ tail is long.
   (horse)

Beginning/Intermediate Read the directions for each section and model examples 1 and 4. Have children work with partners to circle the nouns and complete the sentences. Have them say the sentences to each other.

Name_____

Write About It

Use story details to support your answers. Use the lines below or another sheet of paper.

1. What are the two settings of this story?

   _____

   _____

2. Who helps Cinderella go to the ball? How does she help?

   _____

   _____

Talk About It

Discuss your answers to questions 1–2 and the questions below with a partner or group. Use complete sentences.

3. Think about a time that you helped someone. How did you feel?

4. What inference can you make about the stepsisters and the stepmother? Why did they make Cinderella do all the work?

5. Take turns pretending to be characters in the story. Act out a scene.

Beginning/Intermediate Read the directions and questions aloud. Guide children's written responses. Encourage children to use academic language, such as *character* and *setting*, in the discussion. You may wish to have children listen to the selection on the **Audio CD**.

Listen to your teacher read *Computers– Then and Now* aloud. Use the Compare and Contrast Chart below to take notes. Then retell the information in this book.

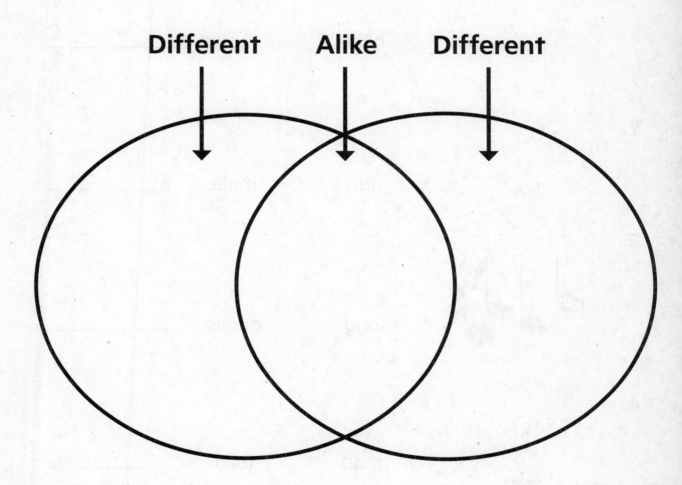

Different   **Alike**   **Different**

Beginning/Intermediate Read the directions. Ask children to pay attention to verb tense and to look at the visual details as you read aloud. Explain to children how and where they should take notes on the chart.

Grade 2 Unit 2 Week 5   55

Name_____

Phonics/Word Study: Long *u*
Circle the word that names the picture.
Write the word on the line.

1.

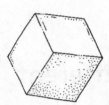

cube   cup   _____

2.

fun   mule   _____

3.

bug   music   _____

4.

mud   tulip   _____

Circle the word with the long *u* sound. Say the word.

5. comb   cub   cute

6. home   unit   hug

Beginning/Intermediate Review how to decode words. Read and point to two words with the long *u* sound (*cube, mule*). Point out your mouth position. Have children say the words and listen to the **Sound Pronunciation CD**.

Name _____

Phonics: Inflectional Ending *-ing*

Add the ending to the base word. Write the new word on the line.

1. enjoy + ing = _____

2. look + ing = _____

3. delight + ing = _____

4. think + ing = _____

Circle the word that completes the sentence.
Write the word on the line. Say the sentence.

5. She is _____ her favorite book.

   read   reading

6. The children are _____ basketball.

   played   playing

7. Kim is _____ to play the piano.

   learned   learning

8. The horse is _____ over the fence.

   jumped   jumping

Read the Decodable Reader *Luke's Tune* with a partner.

© Macmillan/McGraw-Hill

Beginning/Intermediate For each section, read the directions and
model an example. Have partners say the sentences to each other.
Have children listen to the **Sound Pronunciation CD**.

Use the word chart to study this week's vocabulary words.
Write a sentence using each word in your writer's notebook.

Word	Context Sentence	Illustration
allowed _____	We are not <u>allowed</u> to wear baseball caps in school.	**Describe things you are not allowed to do in school.**
powerful _____	Many trees fell during the <u>powerful</u> winter storm.	
invented _____	Thomas Edison <u>invented</u> the light bulb.	
instrument _____	The dentist used a special <u>instrument</u> to clean my teeth.	
products _____	We bought paper <u>products</u> for the picnic.	
design _____	The mittens have a snowflake <u>design</u>.	

© Macmillan/McGraw-Hill

Beginning/Intermediate Review vocabulary. Use gestures to demonstrate meaning. Pair children to write sentences, or draw pictures, to illustrate the meaning of the newly acquired vocabulary and tell sentences to each other.

Name _____

Grammar: Plurals and Possessives
Circle the possessive or plural word that completes the sentence. Then write that word on the line.

1. My _____ house is nearby.

       uncles   uncle's

2. The _____ go to the library after school.

       boys   boy's

3. Your _____ are too loud at night.

       dogs   dog's

Write the possessive form of the plural noun in ( ) to complete the sentence.

4. Have you seen the _____ cafeteria?

       (teachers)

5. My _____ car is in the garage.

       (parents)

6. The baseball _____ bats are new.

       (players)

Beginning/Intermediate Read the directions for each section and model examples 1 and 4. Have children work with partners to circle the nouns and complete the sentences. Have them say sentences 4–6 to each other.

Grade 2 Unit 2 Week 5 **59**

Write About It

Use story details to support your answers. Use the lines below or another sheet of paper.

1. Name three important parts of a computer.

   _____

   _____

2. What are some ways to use a computer?

   _____

   _____

Remember to:

- Ask about words you don't know.

- Retell what you hear to check understanding.

- Listen carefully to your classmates.

- Use gestures to help show what you mean.

Talk About It

Discuss your answers to questions 1–2 and the questions below with a partner or group.

3. What are some machines with computers inside?

4. What did you learn about computers from this book?

5. Talk about ways that computers might make your school day different in the future.

© Macmillan/McGraw-Hill

Beginning/Intermediate Read the directions and questions aloud. Guide children's written responses. During the discussion, have children describe and explain how computers can be helpful in school. You may wish to have children listen to the selection on the **Audio CD**.

Name ______________________________

Taking Notes

Listen to your teacher read *Our Statue of Liberty* aloud. Use the Summary Chart below to take notes. Then retell the book.

Main Idea

Main Idea

Main Idea

Summary

Beginning/Intermediate Read the directions. As children listen to the story, work together to identify important main ideas in the text. Help children use the main ideas to write a summary. Explain how and where they should take notes on the chart.

Name _____

Phonics/Word Study: *r*-Controlled Vowels: *er, ir, ur*
Circle the word that names the picture. Say the word.

1.   girl   gate   grow

2.   fat   fern   feet

3.   hat   hand   hurt

4.   skate   skin   skirt

Circle the word with *er, ir,* or *ur*.
Write the word on the line.

5.   verb   real   _____

6.   burn   bite   _____

7.   cake   circle   _____

8.   herd   hen   _____

© Macmillan/McGraw-Hill

Beginning/Intermediate Review how to decode words. In each section, read and point to one word with the new sound. Point out your mouth position. Have children say the words and listen to the **Sound Pronunciation CD**.

Phonics: Inflectional Endings -er, -est
Circle a word to complete each sentence.

1. That story was the _____ one in the book.

   sadder   saddest

2. This puddle is _____ than that one.

   wider   widest

3. Giraffes are _____ than bears.

   bigger   biggest

4. Abdullah thinks math is the _____ subject.

   harder   hardest

Circle the ending that completes the word in dark print.
Write the ending on the line. Say the sentence.

5. Marie is the **fast** _____ runner in the class.

   er   est

6. Spring is **warm** _____ than winter.

   er   est

7. Bob is the **tall** _____ player on the team.

   er   est

Read the Decodable Reader _Shirl and Her Tern_ with a partner.

Beginning/Intermediate Model examples 1 and 5 and say the words
for children to repeat. Have partners complete the page and read the
sentences to each other.

Grade 2 Unit 3 Week 1 63

Use the word chart to study this week's vocabulary words.
Write a sentence using each word in your writer's notebook.

Word	Context Sentence	Illustration
perform _____	I feel nervous when I <u>perform</u> in front of people.	
effort _____	Learning to play the piano well takes a lot of <u>effort</u>.	**Describe some things that take a lot of effort to do.**
remember _____	I put my piano music by the door so I would <u>remember</u> it.	
mood _____	The funny song put me in a good <u>mood</u>.	**Which would put you in a bad mood—watching a funny movie or doing extra homework?**
proud _____	I am <u>proud</u> of the painting I made for Mom.	

© Macmillan/McGraw-Hill

Beginning/Intermediate Review vocabulary. Use gestures to demonstrate meaning. Pair children to write sentences or draw pictures to illustrate the meaning of the newly acquired vocabulary. Have them say sentences to each other.

Name _____

Grammar: Action Verbs
Circle the action verb in each sentence.
Say the sentences.

1. The elf talks to the woodcutter.

2. He wants some food.

3. The woodcutter wastes the wishes.

4. His wife yells at him.

Write two sentences with action verbs to tell what is happening in the picture.

5. _____

6. _____

Beginning/Intermediate Read each set of directions and model the first example. Have partners circle the verbs and write the sentences together. Have children share their sentences with the group.

Grade 2 Unit 3 Week 1 65

Write About It

Use story details to support your answers. Use the lines below or another sheet of paper.

1. Write a sentence that tells how the Statue of Liberty makes Americans feel.

_____

_____

2. Name one of the people that helped build the Statue of Liberty.

_____

_____

Remember to:

- Listen to the speaker.

- Retell what you hear to check understanding.

- Use the new words you have learned.

- Ask for help if you don't understand.

Talk About It

Discuss your answers to questions 1–2 and the questions below with a partner or group.

3. Summarize the steps the artist took to build the Statue of Liberty.

4. Why do you think Eiffel had to make a steel frame to support the statue?

5. What do you think the Statue of Liberty stands for?

Beginning/Intermediate Read the directions and questions aloud. Guide children's written responses. Encourage them to share their ideas and opinions during discussion. Guide them to use the sequence words on pages 8–9 to help summarize. Have children listen to the **Audio CD**.

Name _____

Listen to your teacher read *Anansi: An African Tale* aloud. Use the Summary Chart below to take notes. Then retell the story.

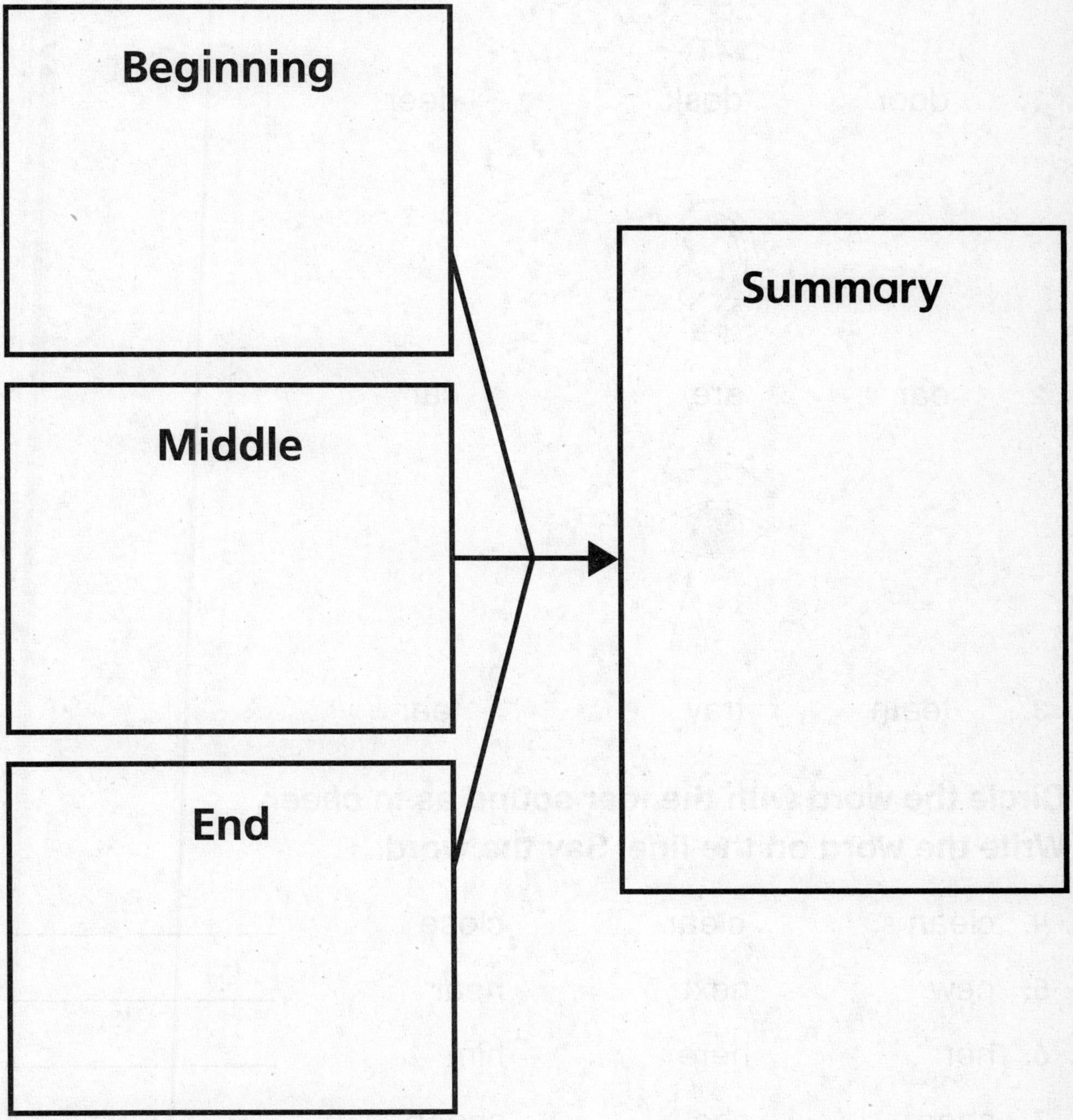

Beginning

Middle

End

Summary

Beginning/Intermediate Read the directions. Remind children to look for key visual details and think about the order of events as they listen to the story. Explain to children how and where they should take notes on the chart. Then guide children to combine their notes for a summary.

Phonics/Word Study: *r*-Controlled Vowels: *eer, ere, ear*
Circle the word that names each picture.

1.   door   desk   deer

2.   ear   are   car

3.   teeth   tray   tear

Circle the word with the -*eer* sound as in *cheer*.
Write the word on the line. Say the word.

4. clean   clear   close   _____

5. new   next   near   _____

6. her   here   him   _____

7. sheer   she   sheep   _____

Beginning/Intermediate Read each set of directions. Model examples
1 and 4. Say each word for children to repeat. Have partners complete
the examples and say the words. Children can listen to the **Sound
Pronunciation CD**.

Name_____

Phonics: Silent Letters

Circle the word that names each picture.
Say the word.

1.   knee   nap

2.   note   knob

3.   gnat   nail

4.    knife   kite

Circle the word with the *m* sound. Write it on the line.

5. test   lamb   curve   _____

6. song   circle   climb   _____

Circle the word with the *r* sound. Write it on the line.

7. write   bite   light   _____

8. apple   wrong   wing   _____

Read the Decodable Reader *Hide and Seek* with a partner.

Beginning/Intermediate For each section, read the directions and model the first example. Have partners say the words to each other.

© Macmillan/McGraw-Hill

Name _____

Use the word chart to study this week's vocabulary words.
Write a sentence using each word in your writer's notebook.

Word	Context Sentence	Illustration
medium _____	I picked the <u>medium</u> ice-cream cone.	
stubborn _____	The <u>stubborn</u> puppy would not go for a walk.	**Does a stubborn person listen to advice?**
noticed _____	Sue <u>noticed</u> a hole in her favorite sweater.	
cozy _____	The cat looks <u>cozy</u> sleeping in the chair.	**What is a synonym for cozy?**
arrive _____	The guests <u>arrived</u> at 1:00.	
argue _____	Sam and Tim <u>argued</u> about who would play with the ball.	

© Macmillan/McGraw-Hill

Beginning/Intermediate Review vocabulary. Use gestures to demonstrate meaning. Pair children to write sentences or draw pictures to illustrate the meaning of the newly acquired vocabulary. Have them say sentences to each other.

Name_____

Grammar: Present-Tense Verbs

**Circle the present-tense verb that tells about the picture.
Then write the word on the line. Say the sentence.**

1. He _____ water on hot days.

   drink   drinks

2. She _____ her book.

   reads   read

3. He _____ his hands before he eats.

   wash   washes

Underline the present-tense verb in each sentence.

4. The girl helps her mother in the kitchen.

5. She plays with her toys every day.

6. He works with an adult in the garden.

7. My mom watches me swim.

Beginning/Intermediate Read the directions for each section and
model examples 1 and 4. Have children work with partners to circle the
verbs and complete the sentences. Have them say the sentences to
each other.

Grade 2 Unit 3 Week 2   71

Write About It

Use story details to support your answers. Use the lines below or another sheet of paper.

1. Why does Anansi trick Turtle?

   _____

   _____

2. How does Anansi's trick make Turtle feel?

   _____

   _____

Remember to:

- Listen to the speaker.

- Ask and answer questions about the story.

- Use the new words you have learned.

- Use your own experiences to help you understand.

Talk About It

Discuss your answers to questions 1–2 and the questions below with a partner or group.

3. Does Anansi act like a good friend to Turtle? Why or why not?

4. Imagine you are Turtle. Would you trick Anansi? Why or why not?

5. Do you think Anansi learns a lesson?

Beginning/Intermediate Read the directions and questions aloud. Guide children's written responses. Encourage children to use their own experiences to help them understand Anansi's and Turtle's actions. You may wish to have children listen to the selection on the **Audio CD**.

Listen to your teacher read *Sounds All Around* aloud. Use the Author's Purpose Chart below to take notes. Then tell why the author wrote the book.

Clue	Clue

↓ ↓

Author's Purpose

Beginning/Intermediate Read the directions. Guide children to identify the topic of the book. Have children discuss how they think this may help them infer the author's purpose. Explain to children how and where they should take notes on the chart.

Grade 2 Unit 3 Week 3 73

Name _____

Phonics/Word Study: *r*-Controlled Vowels: *ar*
Circle the word that names the picture.

1. bark   bake   bean

2. sun   shirt   star

3. shake   shark   sat

4. can   crop   card

Circle the word with the ar sound as in *car*.
Write the word on the line. Say the word.

5. barn   burn   _____

6. cat   cart   _____

7. heat   hard   _____

8. farm   fan   _____

Beginning/Intermediate Read and point to examples 1–4. Have partners complete the page and say words 5–8 to each other.

Name _____

Phonics: Inflectional Ending *-ed*
Write the ending that shows the past-tense form of each verb in dark print.

1. The gecko's skin **help** _____ it hide.

2. I **learn** _____ about animals in the rainforest.

3. The python **look** _____ at its prey.

4. The animals **stay** _____ away from the poison dart frog.

Choose a word from the box to complete each sentence. Write the word on the line. Say the sentence.

climbed	called	jumped	hunted

5. The jaguar _____ all day.

6. The python _____ up to catch the gecko.

7. The gecko _____ off the tree to escape.

8. The top of the rainforest is _____ the canopy.

Read the Decodable Reader *Meg Cage in Space* with a partner.

Beginning/Intermediate Model examples 1 and 5 and say the words for children to repeat. Have partners complete the page and read the sentences to each other.

Grade 2 Unit 3 Week 3 75

Use the word chart to study this week's vocabulary words.
Write a sentence using each word in your writer's notebook.

Word	Context Sentence	Illustration
impossible _____	It was <u>impossible</u> to lift the heavy box.	
treasures _____	I put my new necklace in a box with my other <u>treasures</u>.	
talent _____	I think juggling takes a lot of <u>talent</u>.	
pleasant _____	We spent a <u>pleasant</u> day at the beach.	**What would you describe as pleasant?**

© Macmillan/McGraw-Hill

Beginning/Intermediate Review vocabulary. Use gestures to demonstrate meaning. Pair children to write sentences or draw pictures to illustrate the meaning of the newly acquired vocabulary. Have them say sentences to each other.

Name_____

Grammar: Past-tense Verbs

Read the sentences below. Circle the past-tense verb in each sentence. Then combine two sentences. Use *and*, but, or *or* in your new sentence.

1. I visited the zoo last week.

2. The elephant played in the water.

3. The tigers jumped in the grass.

4. Long ago, people hunted giant tortoises.

_____

Write the past-tense form of the word in dark print. Say the correct sentence.

5. We **learn** about animals that live a long time. _____

6. The elephant **lift** its trunk high in the air. _____

7. I **wait** in line to see the monkeys. _____

Beginning/Intermediate Read the directions for each section and model the first example. Have partners complete examples 2–4. Have each child complete the bottom section and read their sentences to a partner.

Grade 2 Unit 3 Week 3 77

Write About It

Use story details to support your answers. Use the lines below or another sheet of paper.

1. Name some sounds that have a high pitch.

   _____

   _____

2. What is a sound you can hear at your house? Write a sentence telling about it.

   _____

   _____

Remember to:

- Listen to the speaker.

- Take turns speaking and listening.

- Use the new words you have learned.

- Retell what you hear to check understanding.

Talk About It

Discuss your answers to questions 1–2 and the questions below with a partner or group.

3. What are some parts of the ear? What do they do?

4. What are some ways that sounds can make us feel?

5. Why is it important for some sounds to be loud?

© Macmillan/McGraw-Hill

Beginning/Intermediate Read the directions and questions aloud. Guide children's written responses. Guide children to use academic vocabulary as they discuss how the ear works. Prompt them to use context to help them if there is a word or concept they don't understand.

Listen to your teacher read *Eggcellent* aloud. Use the Cause and Effect Chart below to take notes. Then retell the story.

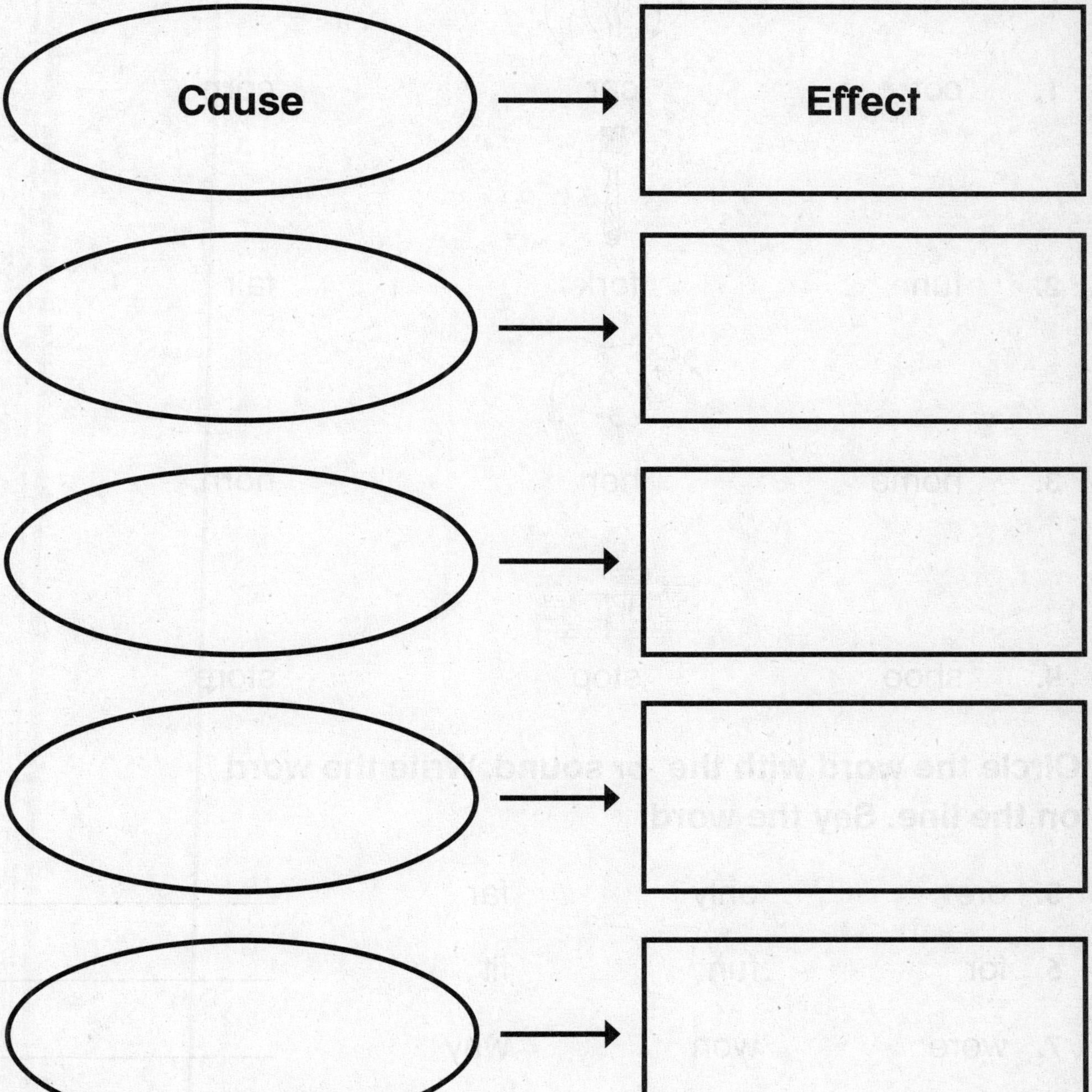

Cause → Effect

Beginning/Intermediate Read the directions. Remind children to look for key visual details and story events as they listen. Guide children to suggest reasons they think some story events took place. Explain to children how and where they should take notes on the chart.

Grade 2 Unit 3 Week 4 79

Name_____

Phonics/Word Study: *r*-Controlled Vowels: *or, ore, oar*
Circle the word that names each picture.

| 1. | cot | car | corn |

| 2. | fun | fork | fair |

| 3. | home | her | horn |

| 4. | shoe | stop | store |

Circle the word with the *-or* sound. Write the word on the line. Say the word.

5. ore   only   far   _____

6. for   fun   fit   _____

7. wore   won   why   _____

8. bear   boar   buy   _____

Beginning/Intermediate For each section, read the directions and model the first example. Have partners say the words to each other. Children can listen to the **Sound Pronunciation CD**.

Name _____

Phonics: Suffixes *-er, -est*
Circle the word that completes each sentence.
Write the word on the line.

1. Plastic can be cut into _____ pieces.

   smaller   smallest

2. Some trash is _____ to recycle than other trash.

   hardest   harder

3. Plastic containers take the _____ to break down.

   longer   longest

Circle the ending that completes the word in dark print.
Write the ending on the line. Say the sentence.

4. The landfill was **long** _____ than the playground.

   er   est

5. This garbage can is **light** _____ than that one.

   er   est

6. That garbage can was the **hard** _____ one to lift!

   er   est

Read the Decodable Reader *More Fun Than a Hat!* with a partner.

Beginning/Intermediate Read the directions and review how to decode.
Read the words and ask children to repeat. Use gestures to demonstrate
meaning. Ask children to practice saying these words to a partner.

Use the word chart to study this week's vocabulary words.
Write a sentence using each word in your writer's notebook.

Word	Context Sentence	Illustration
impatient	Dad gets <u>impatient</u> when the newspaper is late.	**List what you might do when you feel impatient.**
furious	Bill was <u>furious</u> about the mess the dog made.	
neutral	Tom doesn't care who wins because he is <u>neutral</u>.	
emergency	The fire truck rushed to an <u>emergency</u>.	
demand	The police officer <u>demanded</u> that we stop at the corner.	
sincerely	I <u>sincerely</u> liked the birthday present.	

Beginning/Intermediate Review vocabulary. Use gestures to demonstrate meaning. Pair children to write sentences or draw pictures to illustrate the meaning of the newly acquired vocabulary. Have them say sentences to each other.

Name _____

Grammar: The Verb *Have*
Circle the word that completes each sentence. Write the word on the line. Say the sentence.

1. Yesterday Sarah _____ a meeting with her coach.

   has   have   had

2. Sarah and her friends _____ a skating contest every week.

   has   have   had

3. Now she _____ an Olympic gold medal.

   has   have   had

Write *present* or *past* to tell if each word in dark print is in the present tense or in the past tense.

4. Sarah **has** breakfast before she practices. _____

5. Last year, Sarah **had** a lot of fun skating. _____

6. The others skaters **had** fun too. _____

7. The skaters **have** many competitions. _____

Beginning/Intermediate Read the directions for each section and model the first example. Have children work with partners to complete the page. Have them share their sentences with the group.

Write About It

Use story details to support your answers. Use the lines below or another sheet of paper.

1. What problem does Mr. Gomez have?

    _____

    _____

2. How does Ferdie Fox help Mr. Gomez find a solution to his problem?

    _____

    _____

Remember to:

- Listen carefully to your classmates.

- Ask questions about things you don't understand.

- Choose the right words.

- Point to visual details in the story to explain.

Talk About It

Discuss your answers to questions 1–2 and the questions below with a partner or group.

3. How does Mr. Gomez feel when he sees the hens at the cafe? Why?

4. Why do the hens agree to go back to the farm?

5. Go to the Online Oral Language Activities and slideshow for Unit 3: On the Farm to hear more about farms. Share what you learned with a partner.

Beginning/Intermediate Read the directions aloud. Guide children's written responses. Prompt them to use academic language in their responses. Encourage them to discuss the reasons that story events occur. You may wish to have children listen to the **Audio CD**.

Name _____

Listen to your teacher read *Inside Caves: Nature's Artwork* aloud. Use the Draw Conclusions Chart below to take notes. Then retell what you learned in this book.

Fact	Fact

Conclusion

Beginning/Intermediate Read the directions. Remind children to listen and look for key details and events as they listen to the story and make connections. Guide children to work together to draw conclusions. Explain to children how and where they should take notes on the chart.

Phonics/Word Study: *r*-Controlled Vowels
are, air, ear, ere
Circle the word that names the picture.
Say the word.

1. beet   bear   bead

2. can   ear   car

3. cheese   cheer   chair

4. scare   scat   steer

Beginning/Intermediate Review how to decode. Point to and name
the pictures. Point out your mouth position. Have children repeat and
practice saying the words with a partner. Have them listen to the **Sound
Pronunciation CD**.

© Macmillan/McGraw-Hill

Phonics: Prefixes *re-, un-, dis-*
Add the prefix *re-* to the word in parentheses ( ).
Write the word in the sentence. Say the sentence.

1. I have to (write) _____ my story.

2. I will (think) _____ some of my ideas.

Add the prefix *un-* to the word in parentheses ( ).
Write the word in the sentence. Say the sentence.

3. I am (sure) _____ how to begin.

4. My characters will not be (happy) _____ at the end.

Add the prefix *dis-* to the word in parentheses ( ).
Write the word in the sentence. Say the sentence.

5. My friend likes sad stories, but I (agree) _____.

6. I (like) _____ sad endings.

Read the Decodable Reader *The Caring King's Fair Wish* with a partner.

Beginning/Intermediate For each section, read the directions and model an example. Have partners say the sentences to each other.

Grade 2 Unit 3 Week 5   87

Name _____

Use the word chart to study this week's vocabulary words. Write a sentence using each word in your writer's notebook.

Word	Context Sentence	Illustration
creating _____	Dad is <u>creating</u> pictures for his story.	
familiar _____	The story was <u>familiar</u>. I'd heard it many times.	
occasions _____	Birthday parties are my favorite family <u>occasions</u>.	
memories _____	Looking at my photo album brings back good <u>memories</u>.	**Describe two of your favorite memories.**
imagination _____	I use my <u>imagination</u> to write stories.	**When might you use your imagination?**
glamorous _____	I dressed up like a <u>glamorous</u> movie star.	

Beginning/Intermediate Review vocabulary. Use gestures to demonstrate meaning. Pair children to write sentences or draw pictures to illustrate the meaning of the newly acquired vocabulary. Have them say sentences to each other.

Grammar: Sentence Combining

Combine the two sentences to make one sentence. Use *but* or *and* in the new sentence. Say your sentences with a partner.

1. Desi said he didn't know what was happening. He knew.

_____

_____

2. The hens were bored. They did not lay eggs.

_____

3. Mr. Gomez went outside. He saw Ferdie the fox.

_____

4. The hens wanted to have fun. Mr. Gomez was furious.

_____

5. Mr. Gomez said the hens could have fun. They went back to the farm.

_____

_____

6. They were never bored. There were always eggs.

_____

© Macmillan/McGraw-Hill

Beginning/Intermediate Read the directions and model the first example. Have children work with partners to write their sentences. Have them share their sentences with the group.

Write About It

Use story details to support your answers. Use the lines below or another sheet of paper.

1. What would you bring with you to explore a cave? Why?

   _____

   _____

2. Choose a cave formation you read about. Write a sentence telling what it looks like.

   _____

   _____

Remember to:

- Listen to the speaker.

- Use what you already know to understand.

- Use the new words you have learned.

- Point to visual details in the story to explain.

Talk About It

Discuss your answers to questions 1–2 and the questions below with a partner or group.

3. How does a cave form?

4. Why do you think cave formations are called "nature's artwork"?

5. Would you rather explore a cave or climb a mountain? Why?

Beginning/Intermediate Read the directions and questions aloud. Guide children's written responses. Encourage children to express opinions by reminding them they can use phrases such as *I think*, *I would like*, and *I would rather*. Have children listen to the **Audio CD**.

Listen to your teacher read *Wasted Wishes* aloud. Use the Cause and Effect Chart below to take notes. Then retell this story.

Cause		Effect
( )	→	[ ]
( )	→	[ ]
( )	→	[ ]
( )	→	[ ]
( )	→	[ ]

Beginning/Intermediate Read the directions. Remind children to look for key visual details and story events as they listen. Discuss the reasons some story events took place. Explain to children how and where they should take notes on the chart.

Grade 2 Unit 4 Week 1 91

Name_____

Phonics/Word Study: Diphthong *ou, ow*
Circle the word that names each picture.

1. crown   cone

2. bus   blouse

3. couch   coach

4. foot   frown

Circle the word with the /ou/ sound. Write the word on the line. Say the word.

5. towel   tool   tune   _____

6. hole   how   hand   _____

7. moss   mouse   most   _____

8. boys   ball   bounce   _____

© Macmillan/McGraw-Hill

Beginning/Intermediate Review how to decode words. Read and point to two words with the /ou/ sound. Point out your mouth position. Have children say the words and listen to the **Sound Pronunciation CD**.

Name _____

Phonics: Inflectional Endings *-s, -es*
Change each word to mean more than one.
Write the new word on the line. Say the new word.

1. zoo _____

2. berry _____

3. patch _____

4. kite _____

5. baby _____

6. fox _____

7. bus _____

8. friend _____

Read the Decodable Reader *The Missing String Beans* with a partner.

© Macmillan/McGraw-Hill

Beginning/Intermediate Read the directions and model examples 1–3.
Have children work with partners to complete the page.

Grade 2 Unit 4 Week 1 93

Use the word chart to study this week's vocabulary words. Write a sentence using each word in your writer's notebook.

Word	Context Sentence	Illustration
gasped _____	We gasped when we saw the size of the huge spider.	**What has made you gasp?**
attached _____	We wondered if a fish would be attached to the hook.	
frantically _____	Jack and I looked frantically for his missing cat.	
swung _____	We watched as the monkey swung from branch to branch.	
delicious _____	Together, we made a delicious meal.	**What would you describe as delicious?**

© Macmillan/McGraw-Hill

Beginning/Intermediate Review vocabulary. Use gestures to demonstrate meaning. Pair children to write sentences or draw pictures to illustrate the meaning of the newly acquired vocabulary. Have them say sentences to each other.

Name_____

Grammar: Linking Verbs
Underline the linking verb in each sentence.

1. An ox is very big.

2. Roosters are loud animals.

3. The ox was in the field.

4. The farm animals were warm in winter.

Write two sentences. Use a linking verb in each sentence. Then circle each linking verb.

5. _____

_____

6. _____

_____

© Macmillan/McGraw-Hill

Beginning/Intermediate Read the directions for each section and model the first example. Have partners complete examples 2–4. Have each child complete the bottom section and read his or her sentences to a partner.

Name_____

Write About It

Use story details to support your answers. Use the lines below or another sheet of paper.

1. Summarize the three wishes the woodcutter makes.

   _____

   _____

   _____

2. Why is the woodcutter's wife angry?

   _____

   _____

Remember to:
• Listen carefully to classmates.
• Retell what you hear to check understanding.
• Use the new words you have learned.
• Use gestures to explain.

Talk About It

Discuss your answers to questions 1–2 and the questions below with a partner or group.

3. How would you feel if you wasted three wishes?

4. At first, why do the wishes make the woodcutter and his wife happy?

5. What lesson do you think the woodcutter learns?

Beginning/Intermediate Read the directions and questions aloud. Guide children's written responses. Remind them that they can look at or point to visual details to help them answer questions. Guide them to describe how they think the characters feel during the story.

Listen to your teacher read *Road Safety* aloud. Use the Illustration Chart below to take notes. Then retell what you learned in the book.

Illustration	What I Learn From the Picture

© Macmillan/McGraw-Hill

Beginning/Intermediate Read the directions. Point to each picture and help children use context to understand the information. Explain to children how and where they should take notes on the chart.

Grade 2 Unit 4 Week 2 97

Name _____

Phonics/Word Study: Diphthong /oi/: *oi, oy*
Circle the word that names each picture.

1.   coin   cone

2.   toys   two

3.   bowl   boil

Circle the word with the /oi/ sound.
Write the word on the line. Say the word.

4. old   oil   on   _____

5. voice   vote   very   _____

6. fold   fool   foil   _____

7. boy   bow   bay   _____

8. choice   choose   chop   _____

Beginning/Intermediate Review how to decode words. Read and point to two words with the /oi/ sound. Point out your mouth position. Have children say the words and listen to the **Sound Pronunciation CD.**

Phonics: Prefixes *re-, un-, dis-*
Circle the prefix in each underlined word. Then circle the meaning of the word.

1. We had an <u>unhappy</u> time last night.

   not happy   happy again

2. We <u>revisited</u> a pizza restaurant.

   did not visit   visited again

3. We <u>disagreed</u> about what pizza to get.

   did not agree   agreed again

4. Then Mom said she <u>disliked</u> pizza anyway.

   liked again   did not like

5. She was <u>unsure</u> what to order.

   not sure   sure again

6. Her soup came cold. The chef had to <u>reheat</u> it.

   not heat   heat again

**Read the Decodable Reader *Let's Join Joy's Show!*
with a partner. Look at page 10 of the story. Point to posters.**

© Macmillan/McGraw-Hill

Beginning/Intermediate Have partners complete and read sentences to each
other. Tell children they may often see print in the world around them. They may see
calendars, newspapers, and greeting cards. Point to the posters on page 10 of the
Decodable Reader. Read the environmental print aloud and have children repeat.

Name _____

Use the word chart to study this week's vocabulary words.
Write a sentence using each word in your writer's notebook.

Word	Context Sentence	Illustration
attention _____	Sam was not paying <u>attention</u> to where he was going.	
buddy _____	I walk to school with my <u>buddy</u> Jack.	
accident _____	Tie your shoelaces so you don't trip and have an <u>accident</u>.	
tip _____	Washing your hands before you eat is a good <u>tip</u> for staying healthy.	
enormous _____	I felt small next to the <u>enormous</u> tree.	**What is another word for enormous?**
obeys _____	My dog <u>obeys</u> me when I tell him to sit.	

© Macmillan/McGraw-Hill

Beginning/Intermediate Review vocabulary. Use gestures to demonstrate meaning. Pair children to write sentences or draw pictures to illustrate the meaning of the newly acquired vocabulary. Have them say sentences to each other.

Name _____

Grammar: Helping Verbs

Circle the helping verb in each sentence.
Say the sentence.

1. The dolphin is jumping.

2. I have seen dolphins in the ocean.

3. The rangers are helping the dolphin.

4. She has saved many animals.

Circle the helping verb that completes each sentence.

5. Angie _____ helping her grandmother.

   is   are

6. They _____ visited the aquarium before.

   has   have

7. She _____ eaten breakfast.

   has   have

8. The people _____ watching the bears.

   is   are

© Macmillan/McGraw-Hill

Beginning/Intermediate Read the directions for each section and model examples 1 and 5. Have children work with partners to circle the verbs and complete the sentences. Have them say the sentences to each other.

Grade 2 Unit 4 Week 2   101

Write About It

Use story details to support your answers. Use the lines below or another sheet of paper.

1. Write a sentence that tells what you should wear when you ride your bike.

   _____

   _____

2. What should you do when you get on and off a bus?

   _____

   _____

Remember to:

- Listen to the speaker.

- Point to visual details in the story to explain.

- Choose the right words.

- Use your own experiences to help you understand.

Talk About It

Discuss your answers to questions 1–2 and the questions below with a partner or group.

3. Summarize how to cross a road.

4. Why do you think it is important to wear a helmet?

5. What is one thing you can do today to be safe?

Use the new words you have learned. Ask your partner and your teacher to help you tell about the story.

Beginning/Intermediate Read the directions and questions aloud. Guide children's written responses. Monitor and support children's efforts to pronounce new words correctly. Encourage partners to help one another infer meaning from the visual details.

Listen to your teacher read *People at Work* aloud. Use the Sequence Chart below to take notes. Then retell what you learned in the book.

First

↓

Next

↓

Last

© Macmillan/McGraw-Hill

Beginning/Intermediate Read the directions. Point out the photographs that show what people need and what they do at work. Explain how and where children should take notes on the chart.

Grade 2 Unit 4 Week 3 103

Phonics/Word Study: Vowel Digraph /ü/
Circle the word that names the picture.

1. roots   rode   run

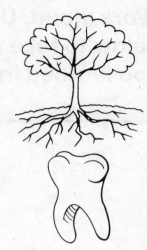

2. toe   tooth   ten

3. fan   friend   fruit

4. blew   box   bend

Circle the word with the /ü/ sound as in *boot*.
Write the word on the line. Say the word.

5. soon   son   _____

6. gone   grew   _____

7. juice   jump   _____

8. salt   suit   _____

Beginning/Intermediate Review how to decode. Point to and name the pictures. Point out your mouth position. Have children repeat and practice saying the words with a partner. Have them listen to the **Sound Pronunciation CD**.

Name_____

Phonics: Suffixes *-ful, -less*
Write the new word on the line. Say the word.

1. color + ful   = _____

2. power + less   = _____

3. wonder + ful   = _____

Circle the meaning of the word in dark print to complete each sentence.

4. The word **fearless** means _____.

   full of fear   without fear

5. The word **painful** means _____.

   full of power   full of pain

6. The word **joyful** means _____.

   without joy   full of joy

Circle the word in ( ) that best completes each sentence.

7. Superheroes are very (powerful, fearful) characters.

8. I like to wear (painful, colorful) clothes.

Read the Decodable Reader *Soon the North Wind Blew* **with a partner.**

Beginning/Intermediate Model examples 1, 4, and 7 and say the words for children to repeat. Have partners complete the page and read the sentences to each other.

Grade 2 Unit 4 Week 3 105

Name_____

**Use the word chart to study this week's vocabulary words.
Write a sentence using each word in your writer's notebook.**

Word	Context Sentence	Illustration
serious _____	The police officer has a <u>serious</u> look on her face.	**When should you act in a serious way?**
personal _____	The doctor was <u>personal</u>. She really cared.	
aid _____	Nurses give <u>aid</u> to sick people.	
informs _____	The officer <u>informs</u> us about bicycle safety.	**What else might a police officer inform you about?**
heal _____	It took a long time for the cut on my arm to <u>heal</u>.	

Beginning/Intermediate Review vocabulary. Use gestures to demonstrate meaning. Pair children to write sentences or draw pictures to illustrate the meaning of the newly acquired vocabulary. Have them say sentences to each other.

Grammar: Irregular Verbs

Circle the past-tense verb that completes
each sentence. Write the word on the line.

1. Yesterday we _____ to a recycling center.

   went   go

2. We _____ away a lot of trash.

   throw   threw

3. A truck _____ the trash to a landfill.

   took   takes

4. The trash _____ down in the landfill.

   break   broke

**Write a word from the box to complete each sentence.
Say the sentence.**

made   had   put

5. I _____ fun planting a garden.

6. We _____ seeds in the soil.

7. The rain _____ the plants grow.

Write your own sentence using each word in the box.

Beginning/Intermediate Read the directions for each section and
model the first example. Have children work with partners to complete
the page. Have them share their sentences with the group.

Grade 2 Unit 4 Week 3   107

Write About It

Use story details to support your answers. Use the lines below or another sheet of paper.

1. What are some goods you buy at the store?

   _____

   _____

2. What is a job or chore you have done?

   _____

   _____

Remember to:

- Share a personal experience.

- Take turns speaking and listening.

- Use the new words you have learned.

- Retell what you hear to check understanding.

Talk About It

Discuss your answers to questions 1–2 and the questions below with a partner or group. Use complete sentences.

3. Why do people have jobs?

4. Would you rather have a job selling goods or a job helping people? Why?

5. How can working together help people get jobs done?

Beginning/Intermediate Read the directions and questions aloud. Guide children's written responses. Guide children to use academic vocabulary to talk about jobs. Encourage them to think back to their own experiences doing jobs if there is something they don't understand.

Listen to your teacher read *Bald Eagle Alert* aloud. Use the Sequence Chart below to take notes. Then retell the book.

First

↓

Next

↓

Last

Beginning/Intermediate Read the directions. Remind children to look for key visual details and think about the order of events as they listen to the story. Explain how and where children should take notes on the chart.

Grade 2 Unit 4 Week 4 109

Name_____

Phonics/Word Study: Vowel Digraph / u̇ / (*oo, ou*)
Circle the word that names the picture.

1. cook   caught   coin

2. bone   boy   book

3. home   hook   hole

4. hood   hope   horn

Underline the word in each sentence that has the /u̇/ sound as in *good*. Say the sentence.

5. You could help Earth by saving water.

6. People chop down trees to get wood.

7. We should use less trash.

8. Would you help recycle?

Beginning/Intermediate Review how to decode. Point to and name the pictures. Point out your mouth position. Have children repeat and practice saying the words with a partner. Have them listen to the **Sound Pronunciation CD**.

Phonics: Inflectional Ending *-ing*

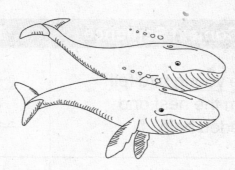

Add *-ing* to the word in parentheses ( ) to make a new word. Write the new word on the line. Say the sentence.

1. The children were _____ in a boat. (ride)

2. They were _____ a trip. (take)

3. They were _____ out at the ocean. (gaze)

4. They were _____ to see whales. (hope)

5. Suddenly whales were _____ near the boat. (move)

6. The whales were _____ closer. (come)

7. They were _____ big waves. (make)

8. The whales were _____ quite a show. (give)

Read the Decodable Reader *Flip and Spots* with a partner.

Beginning/Intermediate Read the directions and model an example. Have partners say the sentences to each other. Point out how to drop the final *e* before adding the ending *-ing*.

Name _____

Use the word chart to study this week's vocabulary words.
Write a sentence using each word in your writer's notebook.

Word	Context Sentence	Illustration
young _____	The <u>young</u> bird fell from the nest and needed help.	
examines _____	The doctor takes her time when she <u>examines</u> her patient.	
mammal _____	Today in school we learned about <u>mammals</u>.	
normal _____	It is not <u>normal</u> to see a whale on a beach.	
hunger _____	An animal will feel <u>hunger</u> if it cannot find food.	
rescued _____	The firefighter <u>rescued</u> the cat from the tree.	**Why might someone need to be rescued at the beach?**

© Macmillan/McGraw-Hill

Beginning/Intermediate Review vocabulary. Use gestures to demonstrate meaning. Pair children to write sentences or draw pictures to illustrate the meaning of the newly acquired vocabulary. Have them say sentences to each other.

Name_____

Grammar: Irregular Verbs
**Circle the verb that shows the past tense.
Write the word on the line.**

1. Alex _____ his sled in the yard.

   leave   leaf   left

2. Alex _____ a TV show about lions.

   saw   seed   see

3. Alex and his mom _____ a new sled.

   make   mad   made

4. Alex _____ the sled race!

   wind   win   won

**Write a word from the box to complete each sentence.
Say each sentence.**

drew	told	rode

5. Yesterday I _____ my bike.

6. We _____ pictures when it rained.

7. My brother _____ me a story.

Beginning/Intermediate Read the directions for each section and
model the first example. Have children work with partners to complete
the sentences. Have them share their sentences with the group.

Name _____

Write About It

Use story details and vocabulary to support your
answers. Use the lines below or another sheet of paper.

1. Where do bald eagles make nests?

   _____

   _____

2. Where are some places you can see
   pictures of bald eagles?

   _____

   _____

Remember to:

- Listen to the
  speaker.

- Ask questions
  about things you
  don't understand.

- Use the new words
  you have learned.

- Point to visual
  details in the story
  to explain.

Talk About It

Discuss your answers to questions 1–2 and the
questions below with a partner or group.

3. Did the law help bald eagles? How do you know?

4. What is one reason the number of bald eagles got
   smaller?

Go to the Online Oral Language Activities and slideshow
for Unit 4: Protecting Earth to hear more about ways to help
endangered animals. Share what you learned with a partner.

© Macmillan/McGraw-Hill

Beginning/Intermediate Read the directions and questions aloud.
Guide children's written responses. Remind children to use what they
read and what they know to help them draw conclusions. Prompt them to
use question words to find out more about bald eagles.

Listen to your teacher read *Saving Sofia* aloud. Use the Fantasy and Reality Chart below to take notes. Then retell the story.

Reality	Fantasy
What Could Happen?	What Could Not Happen?

Beginning/Intermediate Read the directions. Point to each picture and help children use context to understand the story events. Guide children to use their own experiences to decide whether story events are reality or fantasy. Explain to children how and where they should take notes.

Grade 2 Unit 4 Week 5 115

Name_____

Phonics/Word Study: Variant Vowel /ô/ (*au, aw, a*)
Circle the word that names the picture. Say the word.

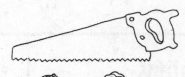

1. set   saw

2. taught   tent

3. land   law

**Circle the word that completes each sentence.
Write the word on the line.**

4. The dog hurt its _____.

    paw   pet

5. Pedro likes to _____ pictures of animals.

    draw   say

6. Who is the _____ of that book?

    actor   author

7. My sister uses a _____ when she drinks juice.

    store   straw

Beginning/Intermediate Review how to decode. Point to and name the pictures. Point out your mouth position. Have children repeat and practice saying the words with a partner. Have them listen to the **Sound Pronunciation CD**.

Name _____

Phonics: Inflectional Ending *-ed*

Add *-ed* to the word in parentheses ( ) to make a new word. Write the new word on the line. Say the sentence.

1. Jay _____ on a team with Mario. (play)

2. Yesterday I _____ they would win. (hope)

3. They _____ to win their last game. (try)

4. Jay _____ the ball. (pitch)

5. The coach _____ to the boys. (call)

6. "You _____ me good playing today," he said. (show)

Read the Decodable Reader *Paul Saw Arctic Foxes* with a partner.

Beginning/Intermediate Read the directions and model an example.
Have partners complete and then say the sentences to each other.

Name _____

Use the word chart to study this week's vocabulary words.
Write a sentence using each word in your writer's notebook.

Word	Context Sentence	Illustration
menu _____	Yum! The picnic <u>menu</u> listed my favorite foods.	**What things might you find on a picnic menu?**
fetch _____	We went to <u>fetch</u> the food from the house.	**Does fetch mean to catch something or to run and bring it back?**
simmered _____	The soup <u>simmered</u> for an hour before it was done.	
assembled _____	We <u>assembled</u> all the food for the picnic.	
devoured _____	Greg <u>devoured</u> his lunch before anyone else.	

Beginning/Intermediate Review vocabulary. Use gestures to demonstrate meaning. Pair children to write sentences or draw pictures to illustrate the meaning of the newly acquired vocabulary. Have them say sentences to each other.

Name _____

Grammar: Contractions
**Circle the contraction that completes each sentence.
Write the word on the line.**

1. The Amazon _____ a desert.

   isnt'   isn't

2. The giant anteater _____ have teeth.

   doesn't   does't

3. _____ fun to watch.

   They're   Theyr'e

4. Tapirs _____ have short noses.

   dont'   don't

Write a contraction for each of the words in dark print.

5. Alan **is not** in class today. _____

6. **They are** hungry. _____

7. My friend **does not** live far away. _____

8. Those children **do not** want to play. _____

Beginning/Intermediate Read the directions for each section and
model the first example. Have partners complete examples 2–4. Have
each child complete the bottom section and read the sentences using
contractions to a partner.

Write About It

Use story details to support your answers. Use the lines below or another sheet of paper.

1. Why does Sofia want to earn money?

   _____

   _____

2. What are some things you have done to earn money?

   _____

   _____

Remember to:

- Listen carefully to classmates.

- Ask and answer questions politely.

- Use the new words you have learned.

- Use your knowledge and experience to answer questions.

Talk About It

Discuss your answers to questions 1–2 and the questions below with a partner or group.

3. What problem does Sofia have?

4. How do you think Sofia feels about the gift she makes?

5. What does Spot do that a real dog can't do?

Beginning/Intermediate Read the directions and questions aloud. Guide children's written responses. Guide children to use familiar experiences to make connections to the unfamiliar or fantasy elements of the story. Have children listen to the **Audio CD**.

Name _____

Listen to your teacher read *The World of Plants* aloud. Use the Draw Conclusions Chart below to take notes. Then retell what you read.

Fact	Fact

Conclusion

Beginning/Intermediate Read the directions. Remind children to listen and look for key details and events as they listen to the story and make connections. Explain to children how and where they should take notes on the chart.

Grade 2 Unit 5 Week 1   121

Phonics/Word Study: Words with Closed Syllables

Put the two syllables together. Write the word. Then draw a picture to show the meaning of the word.

1. kit + ten = _____

2. but + ton = _____

3. pump + kin = _____

4. cac + tus = _____

5. sand + wich = _____

6. in + sect = _____

Beginning/Intermediate Review how to decode. Point to and read the syllables. Point out your mouth position. Have children repeat and practice saying the words with a partner. Have them listen to the **Sound Pronunciation CD**.

Name_____

Phonics: Words with Closed Syllables

**Put the two syllables together. Write the word on the line.
Then match the word to the picture it names.**

1. dol + lar = _____

2. rab + bit = _____

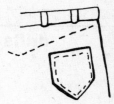

3. muf + fin = _____

4. jack + et = _____

5. pock + et = _____

6. mag + net = _____

Read the Decodable Reader *Judge Marge* with a partner.

Beginning/Intermediate Read the directions and model example 1.
Have children complete the page with a partner and say the words to
each other.

Name _____

Use the word chart to study this week's vocabulary words.
Write a sentence using each word in your writer's notebook.

Word	Context Sentence	Illustration
burst _____	The seed pod <u>burst</u> open, and the seeds flew out.	
drifts _____	A leaf <u>drifts</u> down from the tree.	
desert _____	The <u>desert</u> is hot and dry.	
drowns _____	Do not <u>drown</u> the plant with water.	
gently _____	I <u>gently</u> picked some flowers in the garden.	**When else would you need to do something gently?**
neighbor _____	Our <u>neighbor</u> next door has many plants.	**What is the name of your neighbor?**

Beginning/Intermediate Review vocabulary. Use gestures to demonstrate meaning. Pair children to write sentences, or draw pictures, to illustrate the meaning of the newly acquired vocabulary and tell sentences to each other.

Name_____

Grammar: Pronouns

Circle the pronoun in ( ) that takes the place of the words in dark print. Write the new sentence on the line.

1. **The rangers** take care of animals.   (It, They)

   _____

2. **The desert** is hot and dry.   (It, They)

   _____

3. **Tarantulas** live in the Sonoran Desert.   (They, It)

   _____

4. **The ocelot** hunts at night.   (They, It)

   _____

Write the pronoun *it* or *they* for each word in ( ).

5. (rattlesnakes) _____

6. (cougar) _____

7. (owls) _____

Beginning/Intermediate Read the directions. Review pronouns. Name them and have children repeat. Have children work with a partner to circle the pronouns, and then read the sentences to each other.

Name _____

Write About It

Use story details to support your answers. Use the lines below or another sheet of paper.

1. Name one thing that all plants need.

   _____

   _____

2. What does a plant look like when it needs water? Write a sentence.

   _____

   _____

   _____

Remember to:

- Use visuals to help you explain.

- Retell what you hear to check understanding.

- Use the new words you have learned.

- Ask for help if you don't understand.

Talk About It

Discuss your answers to questions 1–2 and the questions below with a partner or group.

3. Explain how a plant uses its roots, stem, and leaves.

4. How does pollen make fruit grow?

Go to the Online Oral Language Activities and slideshow for Unit 5: Plants and Living Things to hear more about plants. Share what you learned with a partner.

Beginning/Intermediate Read the directions and questions. Guide children's written responses. Review basic and academic vocabulary words such as *roots*, *stems*, and *oxygen*. Guide children to use visuals to help them in their responses. Have children listen to the **Audio CD**.

Listen to your teacher read *All About Tomatoes* aloud. Use the Sequence Chart below to take notes. Then retell what you learned in this book.

First

↓

Next

↓

Last

Beginning/Intermediate Read the directions. Remind children to look for key visual details and think about the order of events as they listen to the story. Explain to children how and where they should take notes on the chart.

Grade 2 Unit 5 Week 2 127

© Macmillan/McGraw-Hill

Phonics/Word Study: Words with Closed Syllables

**Draw a line to break each word into syllables. Say the word.
Then match the word to the picture it names.**

1. cabin

2. ribbon

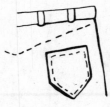

3. hammer

4. wallet

5. pocket

6. napkin

7. princess

Beginning/Intermediate Model example 1 and say the words for children to repeat. Have partners complete the page. Have children listen to the **Sound Pronunciation CD**.

Phonics: Words with Closed Syllables
Break each word into syllables. Write the syllables on the lines.

Example: picnic _____pic_____   _____nic_____

1. tennis   _____   _____

2. channel   _____   _____

3. winter   _____   _____

4. happen   _____   _____

5. basket   _____   _____

6. kingdom   _____   _____

7. hiccup   _____   _____

Read the Decodable Reader _Calvin's Pumpkin_ with a partner.

© Macmillan/McGraw-Hill

Beginning/Intermediate Read the directions and model the example. Have children complete the page with a partner and say the words to each other.

Grade 2 Unit 5 Week 2   129

Use the word chart to study this week's vocabulary words.
Write a sentence using each word in your writer's notebook.

Word	Context Sentence	Illustration
scent _____	Roses have a sweet <u>scent</u>.	**Is a scent something you see or something you smell?**
trade _____	She <u>traded</u> a large plant for some apples.	
muscles _____	He has strong <u>muscles</u>.	
prickly _____	This plant has a <u>prickly</u> stem.	
blooming _____	One flower is <u>blooming</u>.	
aroma _____	I love the <u>aroma</u> of our vegetable soup.	**What aroma do you like?**

Beginning/Intermediate Review vocabulary. Ask children to identify Spanish cognates. Pair children to write sentences, or draw pictures, to illustrate the meaning of the newly acquired vocabulary and tell sentences to each other.

Name _____

Grammar: *I* and *me, we* and *us*
Circle the pronoun that completes each sentence.
Write the pronoun on the line.

1. She gave the book to _____.

   I   me

2. _____ rode our bikes after school.

   Us   We

3. _____ like drawing with colors.

   me   I

4. My brother likes to play with _____.

   we   us

Write a word from the box to complete each sentence.
Say the sentence.

I	We	me

5. _____ went to the library together.

6. _____ don't cross the street alone.

7. My sister goes home with _____.

© Macmillan/McGraw-Hill

Beginning/Intermediate Read the directions. Review pronouns. Have
children complete the page and share their answers with the class.

Name_____

Write About It

Use story details to support your answers. Use the lines below or another sheet of paper.

1. What do tomatoes need to grow?

   _____

   _____

2. How do tomato plants change as they grow?

   _____

   _____

   _____

Remember to:

- Listen to the speaker.

- Use visuals to help you understand.

- Choose the right words.

- Use your own knowledge and experience to help you understand.

Talk About It

Discuss your answers to questions 1–2 and the questions below with a partner or group.

3. How do you know if a tomato is ready to eat?

4. What is a food you like that has tomatoes in it?

5. Would you like to grow tomatoes? Why or why not?

Use the new words you have learned. Ask your partner and your teacher to help you tell about the story.

© Macmillan/McGraw-Hill

Beginning/Intermediate Read the directions and questions aloud. Guide children's written responses. Monitor and support children's efforts at self-correction. Encourage partners to help one another infer meaning from the photos to help them explain how tomatoes grow.

Listen to your teacher read *Living Fossils* aloud. Use the Summary Chart below to take notes. Then retell what you learned.

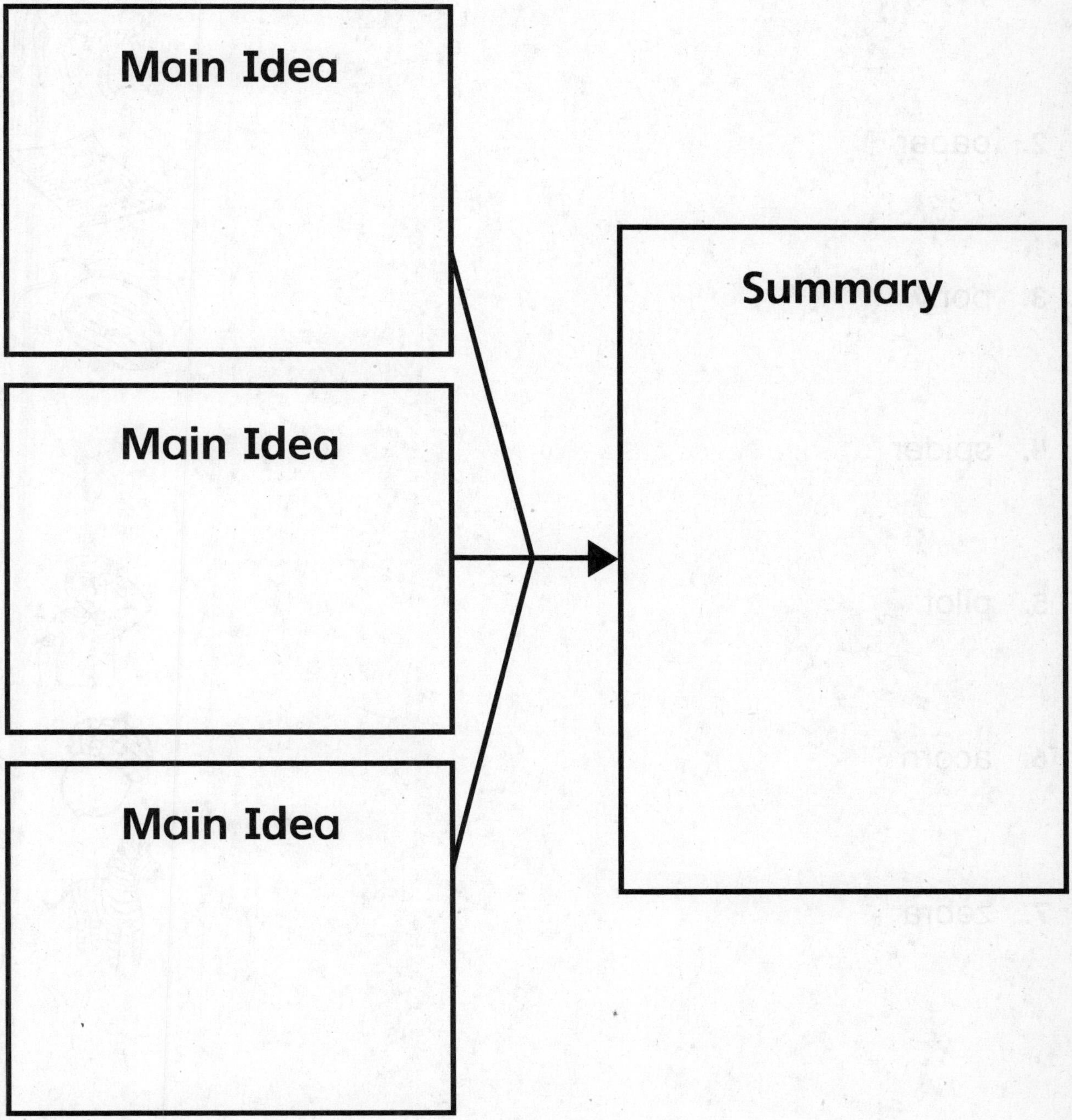

Main Idea

Main Idea

Main Idea

Summary

Beginning/Intermediate Read the directions. As children listen to the story, work together to identify important main ideas in the text. Guide children to use the main ideas to write a summary. Explain how and where they should take notes on the chart.

Grade 2 Unit 5 Week 3 **133**

Name _____

Phonics/Word Study: Words with Open Syllables

Draw a line to break each word into syllables.
Then match the word to the picture it names.

1. yoyo

2. paper

3. pony

4. spider

5. pilot

6. acorn

7. zebra

© Macmillan/McGraw-Hill

Beginning/Intermediate Review how to decode words. Read the directions and break the first word into syllables. Point out your mouth position. Have children say the words and listen to the **Sound Pronunciation CD**.

Phonics: Words with Open Syllables

Divide each word into syllables. Write the word parts on the lines.

Example: lazy   _____la_____   _____zy_____

1. baby   _____   _____

2. tiger   _____   _____

3. music   _____   _____

4. open   _____   _____

5. pupil   _____   _____

6. final   _____   _____

7. evil   _____   _____

8. bagel   _____   _____

Read the Decodable Reader *Decode It* with a partner. Look at page 20 of the story. Point to the code and the note.

Beginning/Intermediate Have partner complete the page and say the words to each other. Tell children they may often see print in the world around them. They may see shopping lists, web sites, and magazines. Point to the code and the note on page 20 of the Decodable Reader. Read the environmental print aloud and have children repeat.

Name _____

Use the word chart to study this week's vocabulary words. Write a sentence using each word in your writer's notebook.

Word	Context Sentence	Illustration
ancient _____	Dinosaurs lived in an <u>ancient</u> time.	
hopeful _____	Carla is <u>hopeful</u> that she will make a basket.	**What are you hopeful of doing some day?**
unable _____	We were <u>unable</u> to visit the museum.	
confirm _____	Use a dictionary to <u>confirm</u> how a word is spelled.	
valid _____	This answer is not <u>valid</u>.	3+3 = 6 1 + 1 = 2 2 + 2 = 5 ✗
site _____	We found a lot of pottery at this <u>site</u>.	

© Macmillan/McGraw-Hill

Beginning/Intermediate Review vocabulary. Ask children to identify Spanish cognates. Pair children to write sentences, or draw pictures, to illustrate the meaning of the newly acquired vocabulary and tell sentences to each other.

Grammar: Possessive Pronouns

Write the possessive pronoun from the box that takes the place of the words in dark print.

His	Their

1. The divers' robot helped them.   _____

2. The teacher's book is missing.   _____

3. The players' uniforms are blue.   _____

4. The boy's bike is outside.   _____

**Circle the pronoun that completes each sentence.
Write the pronoun on the line. Say the sentence.**

5. The children found _____ toys.

   his   their

6. My brother wore _____ jacket.

   his   their

7. Angela saw _____ friend at the park.

   her   their

8. They ride _____ bikes to school.

   his   their

© Macmillan/McGraw-Hill

Beginning/Intermediate Read the directions for each section and
model examples 1 and 5. Have children work with partners to write the
right pronoun. Have them say sentences 5–8 to each other.

Write About It

Use story details to support your answers. Use the lines below or another sheet of paper.

1. What are living fossils?

_____

_____

_____

2. Choose a living fossil. Write a sentence about it.

_____

_____

_____

> **Remember to:**
>
> • Share a personal experience.
>
> • Take turns speaking and listening.
>
> • Use the new words you have learned.
>
> • Ask questions about things you don't understand.

Talk About It

Discuss your answers to questions 1–2 and the questions below with a partner or group.

3. Describe how a fossil forms.

4. What can we learn from living fossils?

5. Which living fossil do you think is most interesting? Why?

Beginning/Intermediate Read the directions. Guide children's written responses. Guide children to use basic and academic vocabulary to discuss fossils. Clarify the meaning of any new words and ask children to elaborate on their responses. Have them listen to the **Audio CD**.

Listen to your teacher read _Little Bat_ aloud. Use the Inference Chart below to take notes. Then retell this story.

What I Read	What I Know

Inference

Beginning/Intermediate Read the directions. Remind children to listen and look for key details and events as they listen to the story. Guide them to use their own experiences and the story events to make inferences. Explain to children how and where they should take notes.

Grade 2 Unit 5 Week 4   139

Phonics/Word Study: Words with Consonant + -*le* Syllables

Draw a line to break each word into syllables.
Then match the word to the picture it names.

1. apple

2. saddle

3. turtle

4. puzzle

5. candle

6. marble

7. needle

8. beetle

Beginning/Intermediate Review how to decode words. Read and point to the first word with the consonant + -*le* syllable. Point out your mouth position. Have children say the words and listen to the **Sound Pronunciation CD**.

Name_____

Phonics: Words with Consonant and -*le* Syllables

Divide each word into syllables. Write the word parts on the lines.

Example: noodle _____noo_____   _____dle_____

1. middle _____   _____

2. little _____   _____

3. wiggle _____   _____

4. dimple _____   _____

5. bundle _____   _____

6. riddle _____   _____

7. circle _____   _____

8. sample _____   _____

Read the Decodable Reader *Puddle Pet* with a partner.

Beginning/Intermediate Read the directions and model the example. Have children complete the page with a partner and say the words to each other.

Use the word chart to study this week's vocabulary words.
Write a sentence using each word in your writer's notebook.

Word	Context Sentence	Illustration
giggled _____	Kim and Rosa giggled at the playful puppy.	**Name something that makes you giggle.**
fluttered _____	A butterfly fluttered from flower to flower.	
peered _____	The cat peered from under the bed.	
recognized _____	I cannot recognize the person in the mask.	
vanished _____	The seal slipped into the ocean and vanished.	
snuggled _____	The baby ducks snuggled together next to their mother.	**What animals have you seen snuggled together?**

Beginning/Intermediate Review vocabulary. Use gestures to demonstrate meaning. Pair children to write sentences, or draw pictures, to illustrate the meaning of the newly acquired vocabulary and tell sentences to each other.

Name _____

Grammar: Contractions

Write the contractions for the underlined words.
Write the new sentence on the line below. Read the sentence aloud to a partner.

1. <u>We are</u> at the animal shelter. _____

   _____.

2. <u>It is</u> on South Street. _____

   _____.

3. <u>We are</u> going to get a kitten. _____

   _____.

4. <u>It is</u> hard to pick just one kitten. _____

   _____.

5. <u>They are</u> all very cute. _____

   _____.

6. Mom says <u>she is</u> ready to pick one. _____

   _____.

7. <u>It is</u> a white male kitten. _____

   _____.

8. <u>He is</u> going to be a big cat. _____

   _____.

© Macmillan/McGraw-Hill

Beginning/Intermediate Read the directions. Review contractions.
Model when to use them. Have children work with a partner to write the
contractions. Then have them read the new sentences to each other.

Write About It

Use story details to support your answers. Use the lines below or another sheet of paper.

1. Why do the birds laugh at Little Bat?

    _____

    _____

2. What are some things Little Bat is good at?

    _____

    _____

Remember to:

- Listen to the speaker.

- Use your own experiences to help you understand.

- Use illustrations to help you.

- Retell what you hear to check understanding.

Talk About It

Discuss your answers to questions 1–2 and the questions below with a partner or group.

3. How does Little Bat help the birds?

4. How do Little Bat's feelings about being a bat change?

5. How do the birds feel about Little Bat at the end of the story?

Use the new words you have learned. Ask your partner and your teacher to help you tell about the story.

Beginning/Intermediate Read the directions aloud. Guide children's written responses. Monitor and support children's efforts at self-correction. Encourage partners to help one another infer meaning from the illustrations.

Name _____

Listen to your teacher read *Look Out for Dolphins* aloud. Use the Inference Chart below to take notes. Then retell about baby and mother dolphins.

What I Read	What I Know

Inference

Beginning/Intermediate Read the directions. Remind children to listen and look for key visual details as they listen to the book. Guide children to use their own knowledge and key details to make inferences Explain to children how and where they should take notes on the chart.

Phonics/Word Study: Words with Open Syllables

Put the two syllables together. Write the word on the line. Say the word.

1. ro   bot   _____

2. e   qual   _____

3. fa   vor   _____

4. gra   vy   _____

5. la   dy   _____

Write the word from the list that matches the picture.

6.    _____

7.    _____

Beginning/Intermediate Review how to decode words. Read and point to two words with open syllables. Point out your mouth position. Have children say the words and listen to the **Sound Pronunciation CD**.

Name _____

Phonics: Words with Open Syllables

Divide each word into syllables. Write the word parts on the lines.

1. motor   _____   _____

2. secret   _____   _____

3. crazy   _____   _____

4. navy   _____   _____

5. frozen   _____   _____

6. human   _____   _____

7. hotel   _____   _____

8. bonus   _____   _____

Read the Decodable Reader *Doggy Door* with a partner.

Beginning/Intermediate Read the directions and model example 1. Have children complete the page with a partner and say the words to each other.

**Use the word chart to study this week's vocabulary words.
Write a sentence using each word in your writer's notebook.**

Word	Context Sentence	Illustration
beloved _____	I hug my <u>beloved</u> grandfather.	
promised _____	We <u>promised</u> that we'd be friends forever.	
wiggled _____	I <u>wiggled</u> into last year's shirt.	
gleamed _____	The ice <u>gleamed</u> in the bright sun.	**Name something else that gleams in the sun.**
glanced _____	I <u>glanced</u> quickly at the dog as I walked past.	
noble _____	The queen looked <u>noble</u> as she sat on the throne.	

Beginning/Intermediate Review vocabulary. Ask children to identify Spanish cognates. Pair children to write sentences, or draw pictures, to illustrate the meaning of the newly acquired vocabulary and tell sentences to each other.

Name _____

Grammar: Pronoun/Verb Agreement

Underline the verb that agrees with the pronoun in each sentence.

1. They (plants, plant) tomatoes in their garden.

2. She (carve, carves) the pumpkin.

3. I (eat, eats) pumpkin pie for dessert.

4. He (washes, wash) the dishes.

Circle the pronoun that agrees with the verb.
Write the pronoun on the line. Say the sentence.

5. _____ buy seeds at the store.

   She   We

6. _____ works in the garden.

   They   He

7. _____ grows pumpkins every year.

   She   They

8. _____ grow very big.

   He   They

Role play with a partner. Ask and answer questions.
Use *and*.

Beginning/Intermediate Read the directions for each section and
model the first example. Have children work with partners to complete
the page. Have them share their sentences with the group.

Name_____

Write About It

Use story details to support your answers. Write complete sentences. Use *and* or *but* in your sentences.

1. Why are dolphins called social animals?

   _____

   _____

   _____

2. Look at the diagram on page 10. Name one part of the dolphin. What is it used for?

   _____

   _____

   _____

Remember to:

- Listen to the speaker.

- Use visuals to help you understand information.

- Use the new words you have learned.

- Ask questions about things you don't understand.

Talk About It

Discuss your answers to questions 1–2 and the questions below with a partner or group.

3. Name one way dolphins are like people.

4. Explain how dolphins find food.

5. How do dolphins help each other?

Beginning/Intermediate Read the directions. Guide children's written responses. Encourage children to use basic and academic vocabulary in their responses. Clarify meaning and pronunciation as needed. Remind them that labels and diagrams can help them as they read.

© Macmillan/McGraw-Hill

Listen to your teacher read *Sonoran Desert Animals* aloud. Use the Author's Purpose Chart below to take notes. Then retell what you read about in the book.

Clue

Clue

↓   ↓

Author's Purpose

© Macmillan/McGraw-Hill

Beginning/Intermediate Read the directions. Guide children to identify
the topic of the book. Have children discuss how they think this may help
them determine the author's purpose. Explain to children how and where
they should take notes on the chart.

Grade 2 Unit 6 Week 1   151

Phonics/Word Study: Words with Consonant and *-le* Syllables

Put the two syllables together. Write the word. Say the word. Then match the word to the picture it names.

1. bot   tle   _____

2. puz   zle   _____

3. rat   tle   _____

4. bee   tle   _____

5. jun   gle   _____

6. whis   tle   _____

7. fid   dle   _____

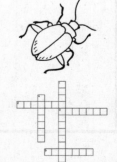

8. cat   tle   _____

Beginning/Intermediate Review how to decode words. Read and point to the first word with the consonant + *-le* syllable. Point out your mouth position. Have children say the words and listen to the **Sound Pronunciation CD**.

Name_____

Phonics: Words with Consonant and *-le* Syllables

Divide each word into syllables. Write the word parts on the lines.

1. maple _____ _____

2. cuddle _____ _____

3. crumble _____ _____

4. simple _____ _____

5. purple _____ _____

6. doodle _____ _____

7. fizzle _____ _____

Read the Decodable Reader *The Camping Trip* with a partner.

© Macmillan/McGraw-Hill

Beginning/Intermediate Read the directions and model example 1. Have children complete the page with a partner and say the words to each other.

Use the word chart to study this week's vocabulary words.
Write a sentence using each word in your writer's notebook.

Word	Context Sentence	Illustration
burrow _____	I saw a rabbit run into its <u>burrow</u> and hide.	**Which animal lives in a burrow—an eagle or a gopher?**
beyond _____	We are not allowed to go <u>beyond</u> the fence.	
warning _____	When a cat hisses, it is a <u>warning</u> sign to leave it alone.	
lengthy _____	There was a <u>lengthy</u> wait to get into the park.	**If a wait is lengthy, is it long or short?**
distant _____	I can see the <u>distant</u> stars.	

© Macmillan/McGraw-Hill

Beginning/Intermediate Review vocabulary. Use gestures to demonstrate meaning. Pair children to write sentences, or draw pictures, to illustrate the meaning of the newly acquired vocabulary and tell sentences to each other.

Name_____

Grammar: Adjectives
Underline the adjective in each sentence.
Say the sentence.

1. Sofia had a good plan.

2. Sofia bought purple ribbons.

3. She made a nice mobile.

4. It was a special gift.

Write an adjective from the box to complete each sentence. Use each word only once.

young	beautiful	silver

5. Sofia bought _____ bells.

6. Sofia had a _____ sister.

7. She gave her a _____ mobile.

Beginning/Intermediate Read the directions. Review adjectives. Ask children to brainstorm some examples. Have children work with a partner to complete the page, then read the sentences to each other.

Write About It

Use story details to support your answers. Write complete sentences. Use *and* or *but* in your sentences.

1. What is the Sonoran Desert like?

    _____

    _____

2. What is one way desert plants and desert animals are the same?

    _____

    _____

Remember to:

- Take turns speaking and listening.

- Retell what you hear to check understanding.

- Use the new words you have learned.

- Ask for help if you don't understand.

Talk About It

Discuss your answers to questions 1–2 and the questions below with a partner or group.

3. Why do many desert animals rest during the day?

4. Summarize how desert plants help desert animals survive.

5. Which plant or animal would you most like to see if you visited the Sonoran Desert?

Beginning/Intermediate Read the directions and questions aloud. Guide children's written responses. Encourage children to use what they know about deserts to understand why living in the desert can be difficult. Have children listen to the selection on the **Audio CD**.

Name_____

Listen to your teacher read *Giraffes of the Savanna* aloud. Use the Animal Compare and Contrast Chart below to take notes. Then tell what you learned in the book.

Animal	Animal	Animal
Behavior	Behavior	Behavior

© Macmillan/McGraw-Hill

Beginning/Intermediate Read the directions. Ask children to look at the visual details as you read aloud. Guide children to use basic and academic vocabulary when discussing the animals. Explain to children how and where they should take notes on the chart.

Grade 2 Unit 6 Week 2 157

Phonics/Word Study: Vowel Team Syllables
Put the two syllables together. Write the word. Say the word. Then match the word to the picture it names.

1. bee   tle   _____

2. thir   teen   _____

3. mon   key   _____

4. rain   coat   _____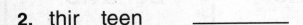

5. bird   house   _____

6. rac   coon   _____

7. cray   on   _____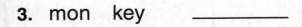

8. paint   brush   _____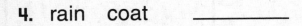

© Macmillan/McGraw-Hill

Beginning/Intermediate Review how to decode words. Read and point to the first three words with vowel team syllables. Point out your mouth position. Have children say the words and listen to the **Sound Pronunciation CD**.

Name_____

Phonics: Vowel Team Syllables

Read the words in the word box. Write the words with the same vowel team next to the letters.

sixteen	roadmap	noisy	away
enjoy	poison	midweek	approach
toy	rainbow	around	ready
Sunday	remain	discount	weather

Example:

ee   <u>sixt**ee**n</u>   <u>midw**ee**k</u>

1. ai   _____   _____

2. ay   _____   _____

3. ea   _____   _____

4. oa   _____   _____

5. oi   _____   _____

6. oy   _____   _____

7. ou   _____   _____

Read the Decodable Reader *The Turtle* with a partner.

© Macmillan/McGraw-Hill

Beginning/Intermediate Read the directions. Then read the words in the box and have children repeat. Have partners complete the page.

Name_____

Use the word chart to study this week's vocabulary words.
Write a sentence using each word in your writer's notebook.

Word	Context Sentence	Illustration
beasts _____	We saw many different <u>beasts</u> at the zoo.	**How are the words beasts and animals the same? How are they different?**
puddles _____	The fox lapped water from the <u>puddle</u>.	
nibble _____	The mouse <u>nibbles</u> on a big piece of cheese.	**Give examples of things you might nibble on.**
itches _____	I have <u>itches</u> all over from bug bites.	
preen _____	My cats like to <u>preen</u> each other.	
handy _____	A step stool is a <u>handy</u> tool.	

© Macmillan/McGraw-Hill

Beginning/Intermediate Review vocabulary. Use gestures to demonstrate meaning. Pair children to write sentences, or draw pictures, to illustrate the meaning of the newly acquired vocabulary and tell sentences to each other.

Grammar: Use *a* and *an*

Circle *a* or *an* to complete each sentence.

1. There is (a, an) sketch in the book.

2. He is (a, an) illustrator.

3. She uses (a, an) computer to draw.

4. Yara is (a, an) author.

Write the correct word from the box before each noun.

> a   an

5. _____ color

6. _____ pen

7. _____ artist

Beginning/Intermediate Read the directions for each section and model examples 1 and 5. Have children work with partners to complete the page. Have them say sentences 2–4 to each other.

Grade 2 Unit 6 Week 2 161

Name _____

Write About It

Use story details and vocabulary to support your answers. Use the lines below or another sheet of paper.

1. Write a sentence describing giraffes.

   _____

   _____

2. How is an okapi like a giraffe?

   _____

   _____

Remember to:

- Listen to the speaker.
- Use gestures to explain.
- Choose the right words.
- Use photographs to help you explain.

Talk About It

Discuss your answers to questions 1–2 and the questions below with a partner or group.

3. What are some things that help keep giraffes safe from enemies?

4. How are humans and giraffes alike? How are they different?

5. What is the most interesting thing you learned about giraffes?

Beginning/Intermediate Read the directions and questions aloud. Guide children's written responses. Guide children to use charts and photographs to help them understand information about giraffes. Use synonyms or accessible language to clarify academic vocabulary.

Listen to your teacher read *Spoiled by a Spill* aloud. Use the Problem and Solution Chart below to take notes. Then retell what you read in the book.

Problem

↓

Steps to Solution

↓

Solution

Beginning/Intermediate Read the directions. Remind children to look for visual details and think about events as they listen to the book. Encourage children to share ideas about how people might solve the problem. Explain to children how and where they should take notes on the chart.

Grade 2 Unit 6 Week 3 163

Phonics/Word Study: Final *e* Syllables
Circle the final e syllable in each word below.

Example: a⟨lone⟩

I. mistake

2. inside

3. invade

4. advice

5. locate

6. excite

7. donate

8. complete

Beginning/Intermediate Review how to decode words. Read and point to the first three words with the final *e* syllables. Point out your mouth position. Have children say the words and listen to the **Sound Pronunciation CD.**

Name_____

Phonics: Final *e* Syllables
Break each word into syllables. Write the syllables on the lines.

1. invite _____ _____

2. amaze _____ _____

3. prepare _____ _____

4. reptile _____ _____

5. outside _____ _____

6. amuse _____ _____

7. tadpole _____ _____

8. vibrate _____ _____

**Read the Decodable Reader *Tadpole Decides*
with a partner.**

Beginning/Intermediate Read the directions and model example 1.
Have children complete the page with a partner and say the words to
each other.

Grade 2 Unit 6 Week 3 165

Name_____

Use the word chart to study this week's vocabulary words.
Write a sentence using each word in your writer's notebook.

Word	Context Sentence	Illustration
conservation _____	Wild animals are safer living on the <u>conservation</u> land.	
remains _____	The crust is all that <u>remains</u> of my sandwich.	
trouble _____	The car's flashing lights showed that it was in <u>trouble</u>.	**What can you do when you are in trouble?**
extinct _____	Dinosaurs used to roam the earth, but now they are <u>extinct</u>.	
hardest _____	The third problem is the <u>hardest</u> one to answer.	**What is the hardest thing you've had to learn?**

© Macmillan/McGraw-Hill

Beginning/Intermediate Review vocabulary. Ask children to identify Spanish cognates. Pair children to write sentences, or draw pictures, to illustrate the meaning of the newly acquired vocabulary and tell sentences to each other.

Name_____

Grammar: Synonyms and Antonyms
Circle the word that is a synonym of the word in dark print.

1. Linda's team won the baseball **game.**

   match   gloves

2. She was very **glad** they won.

   tired   happy

3. The ball was **difficult** to catch.

   sad   hard

Choose the word from the box that is an antonym of the underlined word. Write the word on the line.

tall	light	soft

4. He is <u>short</u>. _____

5. The glove feels very <u>hard</u>. _____

6. It was very <u>dark</u> outside. _____

Beginning/Intermediate Read each set of directions and model the first example. Have partners circle the synonyms and choose the antonyms together. Have children share their answers with the group.

Write About It

Use story details to support your answers. Write complete sentences. Use *and* or *but* in your sentences.

1. What can be hurt by an oil spill?

   _____

   _____

2. How can oil spills make animals become endangered or extinct?

   _____

   _____

Remember to:

- Use visuals to understand ideas.

- Take turns speaking and listening.

- Use the new words you have learned.

- Ask questions about things you don't understand.

Talk About It

Discuss your answers to questions 1–2 and the questions below with a partner or group.

3. Summarize some things people do to clean up oil spills.

4. How can you help keep our world clean?

5. How would you feel if you heard there was an oil spill? Why?

Beginning/Intermediate Read the directions and questions. Guide children's written responses. Point out chapter titles and captions to help children locate information. Guide children to use the photographs to elaborate on their answers. Have children listen to the **Audio CD**.

© Macmillan/McGraw-Hill

Name _____

Listen to your teacher read *The Snowed-Under Sled* aloud. Use the Cause and Effect Chart below to take notes. Then retell the story.

Cause		Effect
	→	
	→	
	→	

Beginning/Intermediate Read the directions. Remind children to look for key visual details and story events as they listen. Discuss the reasons some story events took place. Explain to children how and where they should take notes on the chart.

Phonics/Word Study: Vowel Team Syllables

Underline the vowel team in each word, and divide the word into syllables. Then draw a line to the picture that matches the word.

1. steamship

2. seatbelt

3. footprint

4. mountain

5. greeting

6. feather

7. teacher

8. birdhouse

Beginning/Intermediate Review how to decode words. Read and point to the first word with vowel team syllable. Point out your mouth position. Have children say the words and listen to the **Sound Pronunciation CD.**

Name_____

Phonics: Vowel Team Syllables
Divide each word into syllables. Write the word parts on the lines.

Example:

| shouting | shout | ing |

1. repeat _____ _____

2. tugboat _____ _____

3. classroom _____ _____

4. valley _____ _____

5. teacher _____ _____

6. cartoon _____ _____

Write the words from above that have the *ea* vowel team.

7. _____   8. _____

Read the Decodable Reader *The Rainy Day* with a partner.

Beginning/Intermediate Read the directions and model the example.
Have children complete the page and share their answers with the class.

Grade 2 Unit 6 Week 4 171

Use the word chart to study this week's vocabulary words. Write a sentence using each word in your writer's notebook.

Word	Context Sentence	Illustration
violent _____	The violent storm made trees bend and break.	**Name a word that means the opposite of violent.**
beware _____	We were told to beware of the storm, so we stayed indoors.	**Name something to beware of.**
prevent _____	An umbrella prevents you from getting wet.	
uprooted _____	The storm uprooted a tree in front of our house.	
destroy _____	Our roof was destroyed by the wind.	
grasslands _____	Cows graze in the grasslands.	

© Macmillan/McGraw-Hill

Beginning/Intermediate Review vocabulary. Ask children to identify Spanish cognates. Pair children to write sentences, or draw pictures, to illustrate the meaning of the newly acquired vocabulary and tell sentences to each other.

Name _____

Grammar: Adjectives That Compare
Circle the ending for each word in dark print.
Write the ending on the line.

1. This painting is **old** _____ than that one.

    -er   -est

2. He is the **slow** _____ runner on the team.

    -est   -er

3. Winter is the **cold** _____ season of the year.

    -er   -est

4. I think that strawberries are **sweet** _____ than bananas.

    -est   -er

Add *er* or *est* to the adjective in ( ).
Write the new word on the line.

5. Painting is _____ than drawing. (hard)

6. Her painting has the _____ colors of all. (bright)

7. My book is _____ than your book. (small)

© Macmillan/McGraw-Hill

Beginning/Intermediate Read the directions. Review adjectives that compare. Model how to identify the right ending. Encourage children to work with a partner to complete the sentences, then read them to each other.

Grade 2 Unit 6 Week 4 173

Write About It

Use story details to support your answers. Use the lines below or another sheet of paper.

1. What problem does Alex have?

   _____

   _____

2. Write a sentence telling how Mom and Alex work to solve the problem.

   _____

   _____

Remember to:

- Listen carefully to classmates.

- Use your own experiences to help you understand.

- Use visual details to help you explain.

- Choose the right words.

Talk About It

Discuss your answers to questions 1–2 and the questions below with a partner or group.

3. How is Alex's new sled different from other sleds?

4. How do you think Alex feels when he is the winner?

5. Would you like a sled like the one Alex made? Why or why not?

Beginning/Intermediate Read the directions and questions aloud. Guide children's written responses. Encourage them to think about their own experiences to help them understand Alex's feelings and actions. You may wish to have children listen to the selection on the **Audio CD**.

Listen to your teacher read *Sky Colors* aloud. Use the Problem and Solution Chart below to take notes. Then retell what happened in the story.

Problem

↓

Steps to Solution

↓

Solution

Beginning/Intermediate Read the directions. Remind children to look for visual details and think about events as they listen to the play. Encourage children to share ideas for how the characters might solve their problem. Explain to children how and where they should take notes on the chart.

Grade 2 Unit 6 Week 5 175

Name _____

Phonics/Word Study: *r*-Controlled Syllables

Put the two syllables together. Write the word. Then match the word to the picture it names.

1. tur   key   _____

2. gar   den   _____

3. birth   day   _____

4. tur   tle   _____

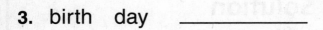

5. bird   cage   _____

6. pop   corn   _____

7. cir   cle   _____

8. a   corn   _____

Beginning/Intermediate Review how to decode words. Read and point to the words with the *r*-controlled syllables. Point out your mouth position. Pair up children to read the words to each other.

Name _____

Phonics: *r*-Controlled Syllables

Match the words in the word box to the letter groups listed below. Write the words on the lines. Then draw a line to divide each word into syllables.

birthday	stardom	cheering	turnip
normal	staircase	careful	perfect

1. ar _____

2. ur _____

3. or _____

4. ir _____

5. er _____

6. eer _____

7. air _____

8. are _____

Read the Decodable Reader *How Bird Was Lured Away from Fire* with a partner.

Beginning/Intermediate Read the directions and the words in the box. Have children complete the page with a partner and say the words to each other.

Grade 2 Unit 6 Week 5   177

© Macmillan/McGraw-Hill

Use the word chart to study this week's vocabulary words. Write a sentence using each word in your writer's notebook.

Word	Context Sentence	Illustration
signal _____	Dark clouds may be a signal that rain is on the way.	**What signals do you see or hear every day?**
randomly _____	The teacher randomly pulled names out of the hat.	
agreed _____	Liz agreed to walk the dog for me.	
gathered _____	Ana gathered flowers from the garden.	**Why might a group of people be gathered?**
jabbing _____	Branches kept jabbing me as I walked along the path.	

Beginning/Intermediate Review vocabulary. Use gestures to demonstrate meaning. Pair children to write sentences, or draw pictures, to illustrate the meaning of the newly acquired vocabulary and tell sentences to each other.

Name_____

Grammar: Adverbs
Look at the adverb in dark print. Circle if the adverb tells *how*, *when*, or *where*.

1. She put the telephone **away**.

   how   when   where

2. The phone rang **loudly**.

   how   when   where

3. I listen **carefully** on the phone.

   how   when   where

4. My brother got a phone call **today**.

   how   when   where

Write an adverb from the box to complete each sentence. Then tell whether the adverb tells *how*, *when*, or *where*.

softly	yesterday	there

5. My friend called _____.
   The adverb tells _____.

6. We speak _____ in the library.
   The adverb tells _____.

7. My shoes are over _____.
   The adverb tells _____.

Beginning/Intermediate Read the directions. Review adverbs. Model the first example. Have children work with a partner to complete the page, then share their answers with the class.

Grade 2 Unit 6 Week 5   179

© Macmillan/McGraw-Hill

Write About It

Use story details to support your answers. Use the lines below or another sheet of paper.

1. Why does the Sky want colors?

   _____

   _____

   _____

2. Why does the Sky begin to cry?

   _____

   _____

   _____

Remember to:

- Listen to the speaker.

- Use illustrations to help you understand information.

- Use the new words you have learned.

- Ask questions about things you don't understand.

Talk About It

Discuss your answers to questions 1–2 and the questions below with a partner or group.

3. How does Blue Jay help the Sky?

4. How does the Sky get the other colors?

5. What color would you like to be if you were the Sky? Why?

Beginning/Intermediate Read the directions and questions aloud. Guide children's written responses. Encourage children to think about their own feelings to understand how the Sky feels. Remind them that illustrations can help them understand and remember parts of the story.

© Macmillan/McGraw-Hill

Pat and Tim

by Liane B. Onish

illustrated by Richard Torrey

Pat and Tim

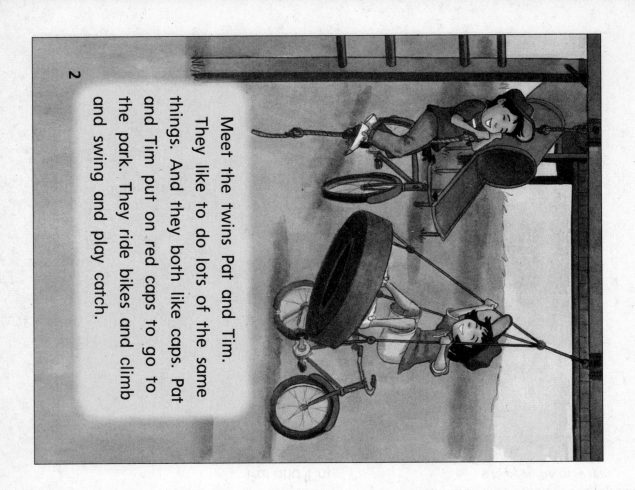

2

Meet the twins Pat and Tim. They like to do lots of the same things. And they both like caps. Pat and Tim put on red caps to go to the park. They ride bikes and climb and swing and play catch.

Pat and Tim

The twins like t-ball. They even play on the same team. Pat and Tim put on blue team caps to play ball.

3

Class 2-P
Miss Pinkham

Class 2-B
Miss Blackwell

Pat is in class 2-P with Miss Pinkham. Tim is next door in class 2-B with Miss Blackwell.

6

Pat and Tim like yellow caps for reading. They put on green caps to study math.

4

Pat and Tim

On Monday, Pat puts on a pink cap. Tim puts on a black cap. But the twins feel sad. Can you think why?

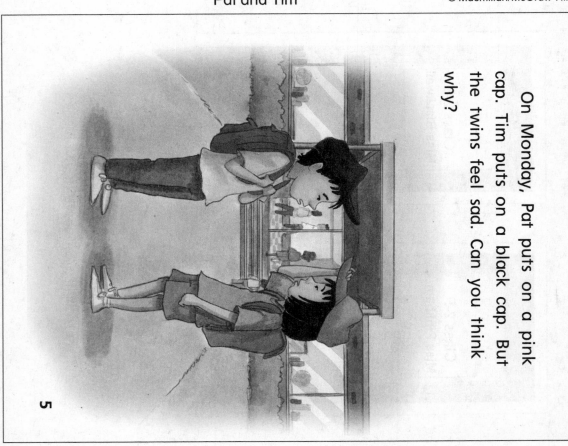

5

Len and Gus

by Holly Melton
illustrated by Bernard Adnet

Gus tugged at the net. He cut the net with his teeth. He set Len free.

"That was quick!" Gus said. Len shook his paw.

"A little friend can be a big help!" said Len.

14

The sun was hot. The sky was
blue. The grass was green and fluffy.

Gus the mouse was on a fun run.
But the fun did not last!

8

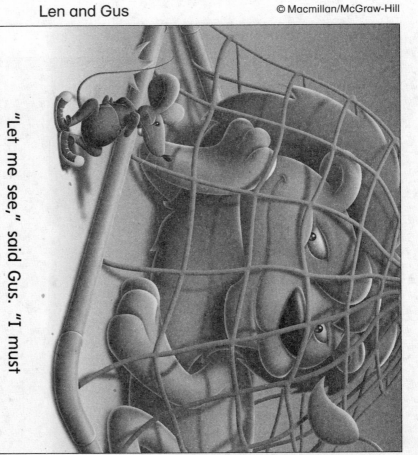

Len and Gus

© Macmillan/McGraw-Hill

"Let me see," said Gus. "I must
study the net. I must find the best
spot to cut it."

"Study fast!" said Len. "Or the
men will get me!"

13

186

"I got you!" said Len the lion.
"A log is a fun spot to hide."

"Let me go! I beg you!" said Gus.

"It may be a lot to ask. But if you set me free, I'll help you some day."

9

Len and Gus

Gus was on a run. "That sounds like Len!" he said. "I bet I can help him. This is a job for a mouse!" He ran to Len.

12

187

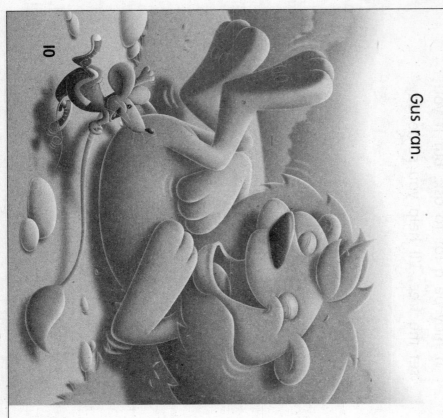

"That is funny!" said Len. "You are not even as big as a dog. How could you help me? But I'll let you go. Run, mouse, run!"

Gus ran.

10

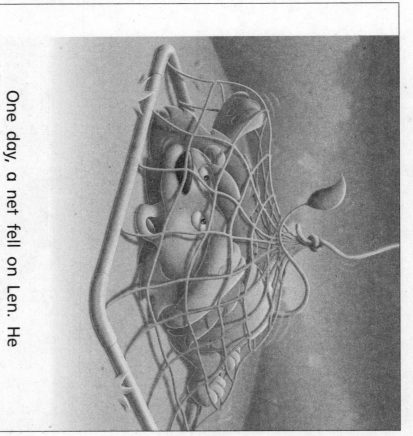

One day, a net fell on Len. He could not get free.

"Men set this trap," he said. "I am stuck like a bug in a web!"

Len gave a big ROAR.

11

You Can Bake a Cake!

This year you and Dad can bake a cake for Mom's birthday. Just get a box of cake mix. Look on the back. It shows you what to do.

16

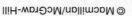

Rub butter on the cake pans. Then shake flour into them. Now the cake will not stick. Next, turn on the oven.

17

20

Bake your cakes until they are done. Let them cool on a rack. Move them to a plate. Add frosting and dab on some red dots. Mom will be glad to see this cake!

Look at the back of the box. Get what you need to make the cake. Put the cake mix in a bowl. Then add the water. This cake has oil in it. Put that in the bowl, too.

Cake

1. Heat oven.

2. Put in a bowl.

1 bag cake mix   1⅓ cups water   ½ cup oil   2 eggs

3. Mix and bake.

18

You Can Bake a Cake!

Crack an egg and add it to the bowl. Then add another. Stir it up so there are no lumps. Put some cake mix in each pan. Dad can put the pans in the hot oven.

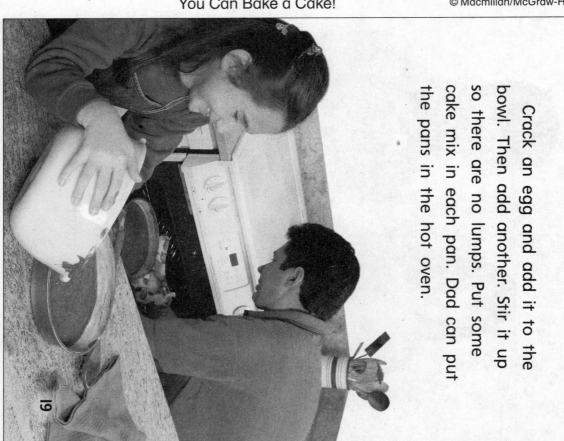

19

Mike's Big Bike

by Elena Matos

illustrated by Joe Cepeda

22

Mike rides his white bike. Each time his legs go up, he bumps the handlebars. Mike likes his bike, but he understands it's not the right size. What will Mike do?

Mike's Big Bike

Mike tells Mom he needs a different bike. Mom will help Mike pay for the bike, but he has to save and help pay for it, too. Mike thinks that this is fine.

23

Mike's Big Bike

Mike rides his new bike on the wide sidewalk. Tim asks to ride it. Mike says, "You ride the red bike. I'll ride the white one. I will ride my red bike another time."

26

Mike gets to work. He wipes the dishes. He rakes twigs. He sells lime ice pops to other kids. He does a number of different jobs. Each dime goes in his bank.

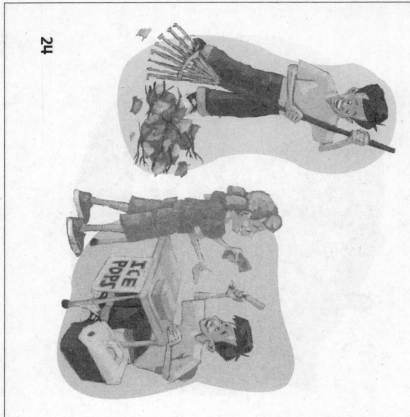

24

Mike's Big Bike

Mike can now pay for his bike. At a yard sale, Mike rides each bike. Then he sees one that is the right size and the right price. Mike likes his new red bike.

25

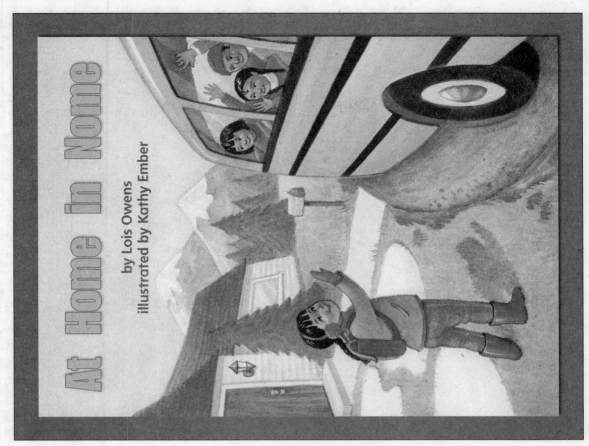

At Home in Nome

May 9

I am in Nome. My family just moved. I have so much to tell. Next week I will go to my new school. I'm scared because I won't know the kids. I hope they like me!

28

At Home in Nome

© Macmillan/McGraw-Hill

198

May 11

It's spring, but it's cold! Some places still have snow. It's not hot like it is back home.

I saw fox tracks in the mud. Dad took a picture of them.

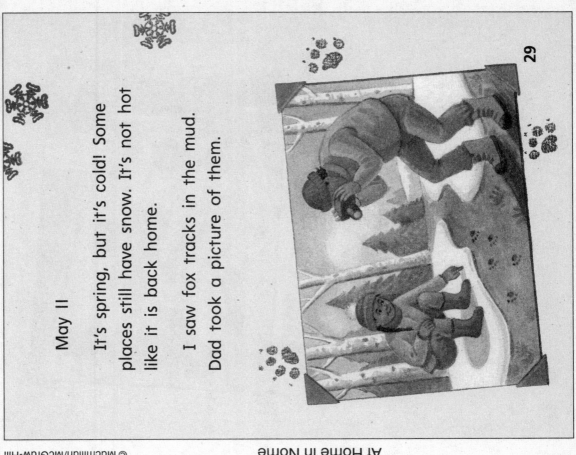

29

June 10

I will like going back home to visit some day. But for now, I am happy to be at home in Nome!

32

30

May 15

Mom drove me to school.
Back home I rode my bike.

All the kids spoke to me! I made
lots of friends. Next week I will
ride the bus. That will be fun!

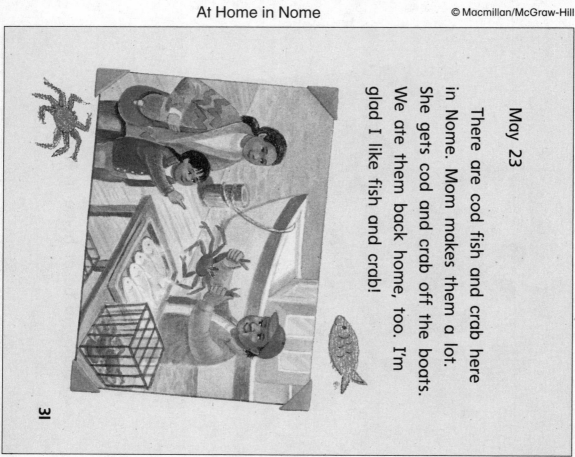

May 23

There are cod fish and crab here
in Nome. Mom makes them a lot.
She gets cod and crab off the boats.
We ate them back home, too. I'm
glad I like fish and crab!

31

Watch the Birch Tree

by Doreen Beauregard
illustrated by Jill Weber

Rich stood still on the stage. He stretched his arms as wide as the world. He clutched the branches.

Rich the Birch Tree was such a big hit!

8

2

In Beth's driveway, a bunch of neighbor kids rushed here and there. They were about to put on a play.

Rich looked at the kids. He often wished that he could act in a play. Then Rich went up to Beth.

Watch the Birch Tree

Beth's dad smoothed the sheet. He cut holes in it.

Beth smiled at Rich. "This is such a good plan! Now we have a part for you in the play!" she said.

7

"May I be in the play?" asked Rich.

"We have no acting parts left,"
Beth said. "But you may pitch in and
help with that cardboard tree. We
must move it to the stage."

Watch the Birch Tree

3

While Beth's dad fetched a sheet,
Rich ran to Beth's yard. He saw two
branches on the grass by a birch tree.
He picked up both branches.

6

203

Just then, Beth's dog America pushed over the tree.

"The birch tree is crushed!" yelled Beth. "The paint spilled on it, too."

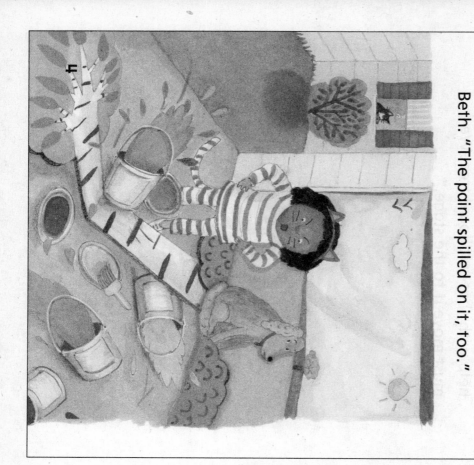

4

"Wait a second. I have a great idea," said Rich. "We need some white cloth."

"I'll get an old white sheet," said Beth's dad.

5

It Won't Be Easy!

by Dorothy Terry
illustrated by Brian Lies

It Won't Be Easy!

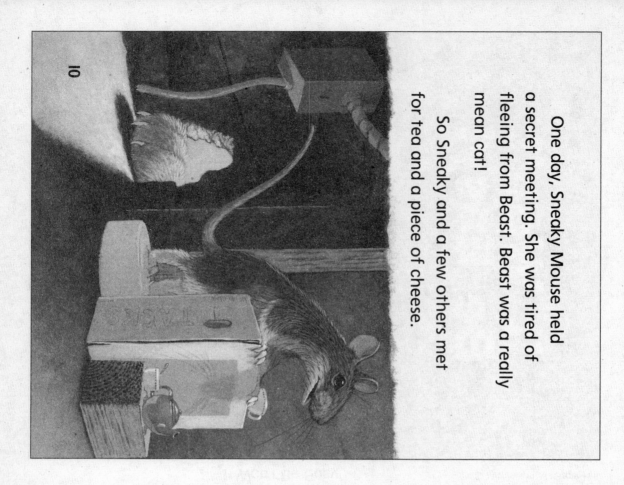

One day, Sneaky Mouse held a secret meeting. She was tired of fleeing from Beast. Beast was a really mean cat!

So Sneaky and a few others met for tea and a piece of cheese.

10

It Won't Be Easy!

It Won't Be Easy!

"What can we do about Beast?" asked Sneaky.

Sneaky asked for any plans. After hearing a few examples, Sneaky spoke.

11

It Won't Be Easy!

Each and every mouse sat still. They looked at Beast. Stanley was right. It seemed that the plan would not be so easy after all!

12

207

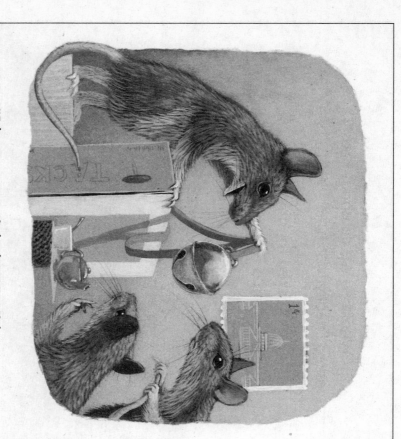

"I have a special plan!" said Sneaky. "It's easy. A loud bell is the key to the plan. We will put a bell on Beast's neck. Then we will hear her before she can feast on us!"

12

It Won't Be Easy!

Every mouse was pleased but Stanley. He sat still between his mom and dad.

"Will it be easy?" asked Stanley. "Please tell me how we will get the bell on Beast."

13

Franny's Rain Forest

by Doreen Beauregard
illustrated by Parker Fulton

Franny clings to a branch with her sticky toes. "I was right! I can find lots of food to eat. It has lots of stuff to see. My rain forest is the very best place to be," says Franny.

22

It is morning in the rain forest. Franny Frog rests in a tree. Franny thinks a rain forest is the best place to be.

"Do my friends like this rain forest?" Franny thinks.

16

Franny's Rain Forest

Franny asks Sammy Sloth.

"This forest can get so hot. But I don't mind! I just go very slowly. I like this hot rain forest," says Sammy.

21

Franny asks Bobby Bat.

"I like this rain forest. I sleep in the day. I fly at night. This place is just right for me," says Bobby.

20

Franny asks Astrid Ant.

Astrid says, "I roam all through this forest as I tow my load. I go from up high to down below. I like all the places in this huge rain forest."

18

Franny asks Alfred Ape.

Alfred says, "I have so much food to eat here! I may eat fruit. I may eat twigs. No place is as good as this rain forest."

Franny asks Patrick Parrot.

"This forest has many bright colors. It's the best place to be," says Patrick. "I see golden butterflies. I see red bugs on branches. I see green flies."

19

Three Goats and a Troll

by Marco Ramos

illustrated by Julia Woolf

Three goats looked at a grassy hill.

"We must eat grass to stay strong. Let's go to the other side where the grass grows," said Joe Goat.

"We have to cross Troll's bridge," said Moe Goat. "Don't wake him."

24

Three Goats and a Troll

© Macmillan/McGraw-Hill

Doe Goat started to cross slowly.

"Who goes there?" croaked Troll from below. "I will eat you!"

"I'm only as big as your toe! Wait for Moe. He is bigger. You will get more to eat," cried Doe.

25

"No, you won't!" yelled Joe. "I will throw you into the water!" And he did.

"My coat is soaked!" moaned Troll.

"So long!" cried Doe, Moe, and Joe. And they ran to the grassy hill.

28

26

Moe Goat started to cross.

"That must be Moe," said Troll.
"Moe will be a good lunch!"

"Hold on! Wait for Joe. He's the biggest of our group. He will be a better lunch," said Moe.

Three Goats and a Troll

© Macmillan/McGraw-Hill

Joe Goat started to cross.

"You must be Joe. I will throw you onto a plate!" said Troll. Then he stepped up onto the low bridge.

27

Luke's Tune

by Sarah Schmidt

illustrated by Ande Cooke

Luke's Tune

217

30

Luke had come from India to live in America with his dad.

"This yard needs green plants," Luke told Dad. "I will grow a few plants."

Luke's Tune

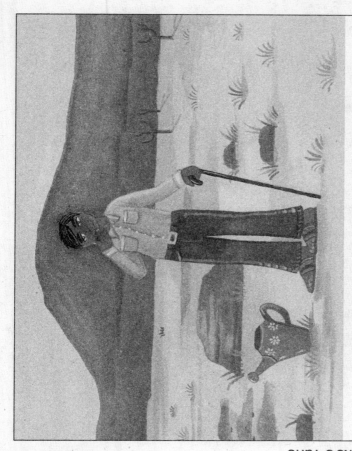

Luke picked a sunny spot and dug holes. He began planting seeds in the holes. Then he used a jug of water to give them a drink.

Luke checked his plants every day. But he didn't see anything.

31

The next day, Luke had a surprise. His plants had grown big and beautiful. It was true!

Luke hummed to his plants every day. Dad helped by playing music on his flute!

34

32

"Why won't my plants grow?" said Luke. "In my country, plants grow big and beautiful. What can I do?"

Luke sat on a huge rock to think.

"It is not fun to plant seeds in this part of the world," said Luke.

Luke started to hum a tune. He liked to hum when he was thinking.

33

Shirl and Her Tern

by Barbara A. Donovan

illustrated by Barry Ablett

Shirl and her Tern

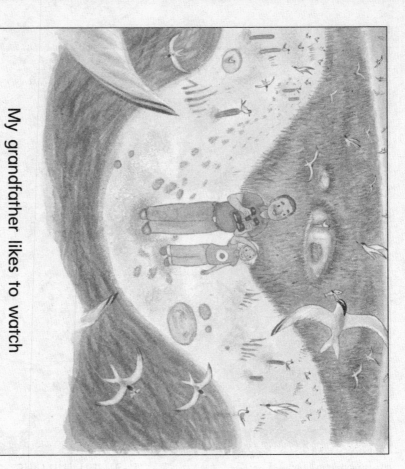

My grandfather likes to watch birds. Each week we find a different area of Burns Beach to spot them. I like terns the best. When they swirl in the sky, it's like a bird show. I would pay money to see a tern show!

2

Shirl and her Tern

Waves churn on the beach where the terns feed. In the spring, we try to keep the gulls out of the tern nests. In the fall, we feel sad when they fly away.

By last week, we thought the last tern had flown away. Then, from the reeds, I heard a weak chirp.

3

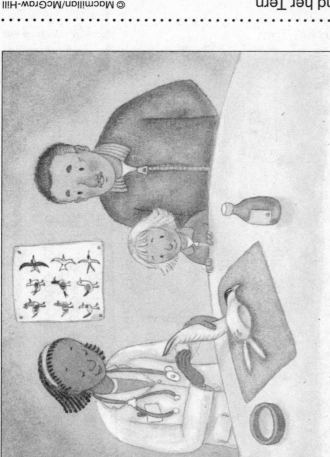

Fern checked my tern. She saw a cut under its wing. She rubbed medicine on the cut to kill germs.

Today I heard good news. My tern is fine! In the spring, it will be with the other terns when they return.

6

We turned toward the sound. We parted the reeds and found a tern in the dirt. It was hurt. It didn't stir a bit.

Grandfather called Fern. She is a scientist and an animal doctor. Fern said to bring the bird to her office building on First Street.

4

We found a box, and we used a piece of old shirt to make a bed. We put the bird in the bed. Then we turned, ran to the car, and drove to see Fern. As we drove, I urged the tern to get well.

5

Hide and Seek

by Liane B. Onish

illustrated by Deborah Melmon

Hide and Seek

Dot went inside the house.

"What happened, dear?" asked Mom.

"The big kids call me Spots!"
Dot said, two tears running down
her cheeks.

8

9

Mom said, "Cheer up, Dot. All young deer have spots. Spots can be most useful. Wait and see!"

So Dot went back out to play. The big deer started a game of Hide and Seek. Fay was It.

Hide and Seek

12

Fay said, "Next year you will be bigger. And you will not have any spots. Then we will play again and see who wins!"

Doe hid behind a tree. But her
tail stuck out. Fay found her.
Ray hid behind a bush. But his
horns stuck up. Fay found him, too.
Dot lay down in the tall grass.
Fay could not find her.

10

At last, Fay gave up. "Where is
Dot? Come out, Dot. You win!"
"Here I am!" said Dot standing
up right near them. "I win, thanks
to my spots!"

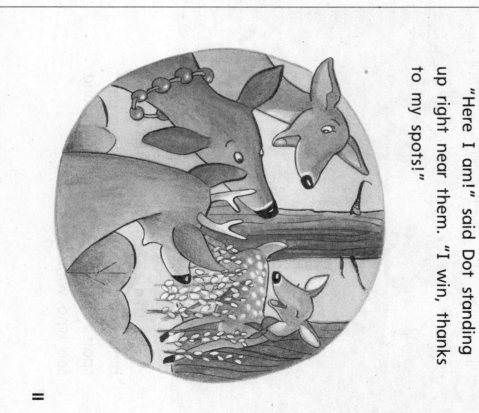

11

Meg Cage
in Space

by Marco Ramos

Illustrated by Dianne Greenseid

Meg Cage in Space

At Meg's spaceship job, it was a slow day. The cold wind was gusting. Few people would be traveling far into space that day.

Meg petted her cat, Parker. Then the door flew open. A big dog raced in, wagging its tail.

14

Meg Cage in Space

© Macmillan/McGraw-Hill

After the dog came a little girl and a man with a big scarf behind her.

"We've got to go to the Moon today," said the man. "Can you take us that far into space?"

Meg didn't think twice. "Yes, I can!" she said.

Meg Cage in Space

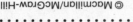

"We named that comet Pig," Meg said as she zigzagged by it.

Soon, the Moon's space manager called. He pointed out a place to land.

The girl gave Meg a big hug and said that it was a marvelous trip. A smile lit up Meg's face. It was another job well done!

18

Meg and her passengers charged out to the field and got inside Meg's new spaceship. She glanced at the flag and saw that the wind was still gusting.

Meg was certain that there would be no problems. She urged her passengers to buckle up.

16

Meg Cage in Space

Meg gave her spaceship some gas and it gained speed. She said, "When we reach six hundred miles per hour, I'll get us some treats."

As Meg got the snacks, a large comet zoomed by the window.

17

More Fun Than a Hat!

a Hat!

More Fun Than

by Mark Melillo

illustrated by Alexandra Wallner

More Fun Than a Hat!

20

When it's cold outside, how can you keep your ears warm? Pulling a wool hat over them can fix the problem.

Before wool hats were made, people wrapped wool scarves around their ears. For some, the wool was too itchy.

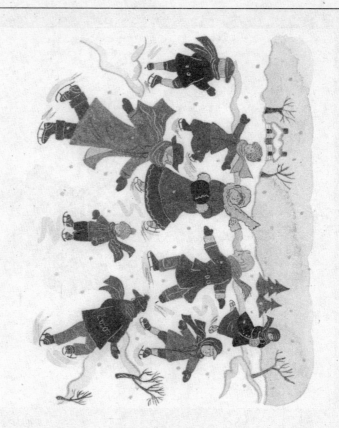

More Fun Than a Hat!

21

That was the problem for Chester Greenwood. His family lived in a region where the winter winds roared. Chester wore a wool scarf, but it was too itchy. His bulky scarf made ice-skating a real chore.

One day Chester's ears got so sore and cold that he could not skate. So he came up with a grand plan.

Chester was just 15 when he came up with his idea! He went on to make more things that could help people.

It was many years ago that Chester invented earmuffs. But the town where he grew up still has a parade every year for his birthday.

Chester thought of a new way to keep his ears warm. All it took was a bit of beaver fur, black velvet, and thin metal strips.

Chester took these things to his grandma. He asked her to stitch them together to make something that would keep his ears warm in the cold.

22

© Macmillan/McGraw-Hill

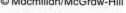

Chester's ear-warming system worked. The other kids wished they had a pair. Still, Chester thought his earmuffs could be better. He did not like how they flapped around.

A short time later, Chester made some changes to his earmuffs. The new ones weren't heavy and could be folded. It was easy to carry them around. Chester's earmuffs were a hit!

23

236

The Caring King's Fair Wish

by Jen Roberts

illustrated by Capucine Mazille

Once upon a time, a king lived in a grand palace. In the palace yard, the king had a garden. The large garden was filled with rare roses. The king shared his fine life with his child, Martha.

The king was a good man. He cared about all the people in his land. He had all he could wish for. But still he wished he had more.

The Caring King's Fair Wish

One day the king was in his garden. He was startled by a man wearing a cloak who was sitting there.

"Why are you in my garden?" asked the king. "Talk to me."

"I was getting some fresh air as I walked among the roses," said the man. "But then I felt ill and had to rest. I am far from home."

27

Martha ran to him. As he patted her hair, she turned to gold!

"Now I know that happiness can't be bought with gold," wailed the king. The man knew the king was sad. He agreed to undo the king's wish.

"Thank you!" said the king. "I will never be so greedy again."

30

The king decided to take care of the man. When the man felt well, he went home. The next week the man came back.

"I have the power to grant wishes," he said. "To repay your kindness, I will grant you a wish."

"I want all that I touch to turn to gold!" said the king.

"That's a fair wish," said the man.

28

The king began to touch things. Soon he had gold chairs, gold stairs, gold rugs, and gold jars! He had all the gold he could carry.

When he picked a rose, it turned to gold, and its sweet smell was gone.

At lunch all the king's food and drink turned to gold in his mouth. Scared, the king started to weep.

29

The Missing String Beans

Detective Split strode up to Susie
Sprout. She stated, "I hear that you
have a big problem now."

"It's my string beans!" howled
Susie Sprout. "My string beans are
missing!"

2

The Missing String Beans

3

Detective Split scratched her head and frowned. "Tell me about this string bean problem."

Susie Sprout cried, "I came out to sprinkle my pretty plants. I saw that just one little green bean was left!"

The Missing String Beans   © Macmillan/McGraw-Hill

At home, young Steve Sprout streaked from the house. He said, "Dad invited Detective Split to stay with our family for string bean soup."

Detective Split jotted, "Case closed," and said, "Splendid!"

Detective Split scrawled notes on her pad. She said, "I see brown tracks that go to the stream. Let's take a stroll and see if the robber is there." So that's what they did.

4

The Missing String Beans

At the stream Susie Sprout screamed, "Step back. Look out for the mud!" But Detective Split slipped, and her body landed with a wet splash. Detective Split cried, "I see no string beans in here."

5

Let's Join Joy's Show!

Let's Join
Joy's
Show!

by Mel Rabin
illustrated by Stacey Schuett

Joy tells the best jokes of any girl or boy in the class. No one can hear Joy's jokes without laughing.

Just last week Joy was hanging out with several friends. The group was having a lot of fun.

8

Let's Join Joy's Show!

© Macmillan/McGraw-Hill

"I don't want to spoil a good time," Joy said, "but I just had an idea. Let's plan a show! I can tell jokes, Beth can play drums, and Troy can sing!"

The kids all started to speak at the same time. It was so noisy!

9

Let's Join Joy's Show!

Boy, did the kids laugh and make noise at Joy's jokes! Mr. Floyd clapped, too.

The show was a big hit because of Joy and a lot of fun kids!

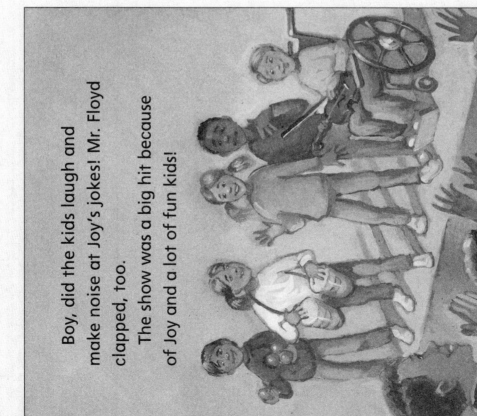

12

Troy and I put up posters, and lots of kids asked to join the show. Mr. Floyd said that he would help.

On the day of the show, it rained and the wind blew. When it was time to start, Joy and her family weren't there! Beth played her drums, Troy sang, but still Joy did not show up!

10

"Joy! Joy! We want Joy's jokes!" the kids chanted.

"Where is she?" Mr. Floyd asked. Then a boy pointed at the door. There stood Joy! She dripped with rain, but she was all set to make us laugh!

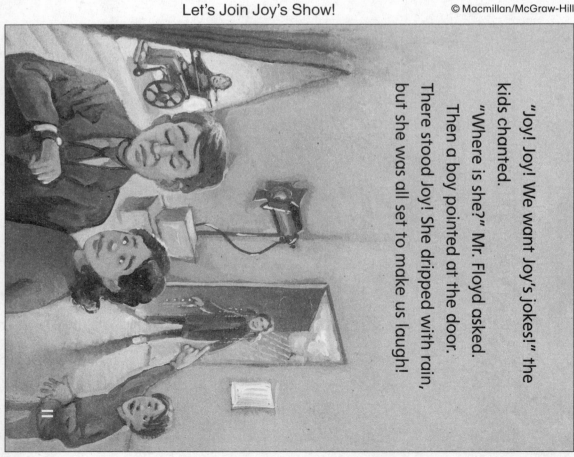

11

Soon the North Wind Blew

by Maureen Shur
illustrated by Anna Vojtech

Soon the North Wind Blew

He took in a few deep gulps
of air and blew with all his might.
He blew and blew till the man's
coat blew out of sight!

20

One day the North Wind and the Sun talked about which was stronger.

"Don't be foolish, Sun," said the Wind. "Did you forget about the time I blew off that roof during a storm?" he asked. "It is true. I am much stronger."

14

Soon the North Wind Blew

"Well," said the Moon, "I watched the whole thing. I think we have a winner. The Sun is stronger than the North Wind."

The North Wind was in a bad mood. There was only one thing that would make him feel good.

19

"But did you forget about the time I dried up all the water to make that desert?" said the Sun. "I'm sure I am truly stronger."

This went on morning, noon, and night. The Moon heard it all and grew sick of it.

Soon the North Wind Blew

15

Next the Sun shone down on the man. Soon the man was oozing with heat and sat down to rest. He took a rock out of his shoe and then walked on. But soon he was so hot that he threw off his coat.

18

16

"I have a plan," said the Moon.

The Moon was wise, so the Wind and the Sun said they would hear her plan.

"Do you see that man in the suit?" asked the Moon. "The stronger of you will get him to take off his coat. That will be the proof we need."

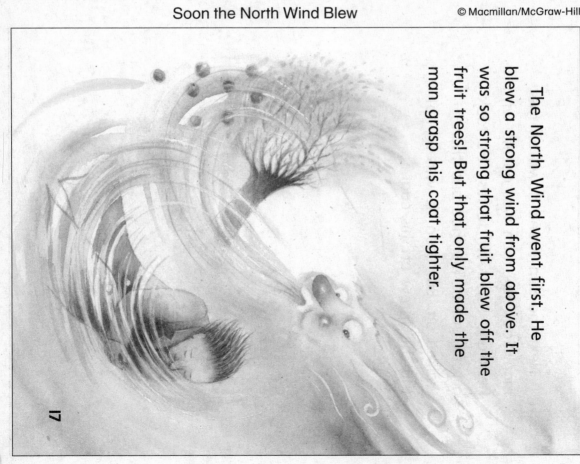

Soon the North Wind Blew

The North Wind went first. He blew a strong wind from above. It was so strong that fruit blew off the fruit trees! But that only made the man grasp his coat tighter.

17

Flip and Spots

by Sandy Riggs

illustrated by Dani Jones

Flip and Spots

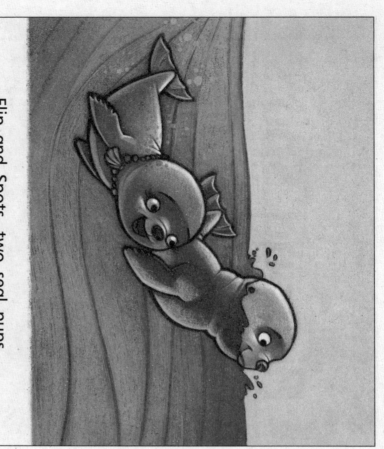

22

Flip and Spots, two seal pups, were swimming in the sea. The pups were swimming just below the top of the water.

Then Flip popped his head out of the water to look around.

Flip and Spots

"Let's go on the rocks," Flip said
to Spots. "It would feel good to lie
in the sun."

Both pups climbed on the rocks.

"Look," Spots said. "The people
from the city are looking at us."

23

26

The people clapped. So the
pups rolled over again. The people
cheered. So the pups rolled over
five more times!

"You are so cute!" a girl cried.
The pups smiled and bowed.

Then Flip yelled to the people, "Look at me." He shook his head. He slapped the water with a flipper.

"Look at us," Spots shouted. Then both pups rolled over with their flippers in the air.

25

"We should do tricks," Spots said. "I can do a trick with this ball. I own it. I gave Fin Whale three fish for it."

Spots set the ball on her nose. It did not roll off. "Wow!" Flip said. "I wish I could do that."

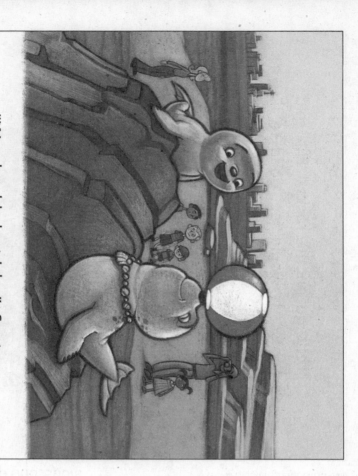

24

Paul Saw
Arctic Foxes

by Maryann Dobeck
illustrated by Bob Dacey

Paul Saw Arctic Foxes

Paul yawned and crawled out of bed at dawn. As he ate his toast, he saw the sunrise. He did not have time for a complete meal.

Paul grabbed his coat and his camera. He walked out into the cold, treeless Arctic land.

28

Paul Saw Arctic Foxes

© Macmillan/McGraw-Hill

When Paul was a boy, he saw a TV show about Arctic foxes. That launched Paul's study of the foxes. He had a lot of questions about them.

As a grown man, Paul's job was to study animals and take pictures of them in the wild.

The little foxes yawned and looked sleepy. Soon they would crawl back into the den.

It was time for Paul to go to his home in the city. He had pictures to print! Those pictures would help him study the life of the Arctic foxes.

32

It was spring, but it was still cold and raw outside. Paul's job taught him that Arctic days might be fine or awful.

Paul had good luck. He glanced below and saw what he was looking for—Arctic foxes and their cubs.

30

The mother fox watched her cubs eat. The father fox had caught food for them. The cubs chewed on the meat.

Paul could not measure for sure, but he thought the foxes were 20 feet away. He hauled out his camera and took a picture.

31

Judge Marge

by Rosa Acosta
illustrated by Deirdre Betteridge

Judge Marge

Marge judged the contest. She gave one boy the prize.

"Being a judge is too hard," said Marge. She leaned against the stage.

Marge made a new pledge. "Next year I will make fudge and pies," she said. "I will knit hats and mittens. That will be fun. And it will be easier than being a judge!"

8

2

It was the first day of the county fair. Usually, Marge made fudge and pies for the cooking contests. She knitted hats and mittens for the knitting contest. She got lots of prizes every year.

This year Marge had made a pledge. "I decided I will not enter any contests," she said. "This time I am just going to have fun!"

Marge judged the hats and mittens. Then she sat down near a stage.

"Who makes the best bird sounds?" asked a man. "Marge, will you be the judge?"

A boy chirped. Lots of birds flew to the stage. Birds landed on Marge. They liked her fringe and the bits of pie and fudge.

7

Marge went into a large room.

"Now I can just watch the fudge contest," she said. "I do not have to do a thing!"

A man with a badge rushed up. "Please help us, Marge!" he cried.

"We do not have a judge for the contest. You always made the best fudge. I bought lots of it. Will you be the judge?"

"OK," said Marge. "But then I'll relax."

"We need you to judge hats and mittens," said Mrs. Ridge.

Before Marge could say a thing, Mrs. Ridge wedged a hat on her head. It was tight and had lots of fringe.

"Do you like it?" asked Mrs. Ridge.

"Help!" said Marge. "I can't judge hats and mittens if I can't see them!"

6

Marge tasted so much fudge that
her tummy bulged. She gave the first
prize to Mrs. Strange.

"Now I will have fun," said Marge.

"Marge, we need you!" cried Mrs.
Cage. "We do not have a judge for the
pie contest. Will you do it? Your pies
were always the best!"

"That's true," said Marge. "I will
judge the pies. THEN I will have fun."

4

© Macmillan/McGraw-Hill

Marge tasted half the pies. Her
tummy bulged more. She tasted the rest
of the pies. Then she gave out the prizes.

"I feel huge," groaned Marge.
"I never want to look at a wedge of
pie again!"

Marge went into another room.
She started to look at hats and mittens.
Mrs. Ridge charged up to her. She had
on a badge.

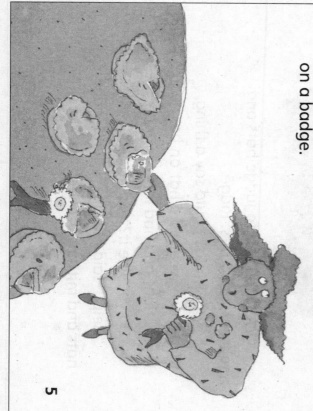

5

Calvin's Pumpkin

by Sandy Riggs
illustrated by Wednesday Kirwan

Calvin and his mom had planted pumpkin seeds. Now they were looking at rows and rows of pumpkins in the field.

"There must be a hundred pumpkins!" Calvin said.

10

Calvin's Pumpkin

Calvin's Pumpkin

"Did you hear about the farm fair?" his mom asked. "There will be a pumpkin contest. The biggest pumpkin will win a prize."

Calvin ran out to the field.

"I think I can find a big pumpkin for the fair!" he shouted.

"I'm certain you can find a very big pumpkin," Mom said.

Soon a man said, "It has a crack. But it is the biggest pumpkin of all. Calvin wins first prize!" Calvin grinned a very big grin!

After a while, Mom, Dad, and Calvin went home. Dad made a very big pumpkin pie! Everyone ate a sandwich. Then everyone ate a very big slice of pumpkin pie!

It did not take Calvin long to find a big pumpkin. "Look at this pumpkin," Calvin yelled to Mom. "It's huge!"

Mom helped Calvin roll the huge pumpkin to Dad's truck. Dad put the pumpkin in the back of the truck. Then Mom, Dad, and Calvin went to the fair.

12

At the fair, Dad drove over a big bump. Bang! The back of the truck opened. Calvin's pumpkin rolled out! It broke into two parts.

"Well," said Mom. "Let's try to put the parts together." So they did it. They pressed the parts together and made a whole pumpkin!

13

Decode It

by Liane B. Onish

illustrated by Holli Conger

Decode It

Irene moved her violin case off the table. Noah, the new boy, sat down and opened his lunchbox. So did Irene. Inside, she found a note. "Who's that from?" asked Noah.

Decode It

17

Irene said, "My mom. She writes me notes to remind me of stuff. She often writes them in a secret code."

"You can read that?" he asked.

"Not yet," said Irene. "Today is Friday. So the secret code is plus 5. Let me show you."

© Macmillan/McGraw-Hill

---

a. 5
b. 6
c. 7
d. 8
e. 9
f. 10
g. 11
h. 12
i. 13
j. 14
k. 15
l. 16
m. 17
n. 18
o. 19
p. 20
q. 21
r. 22
s. 23
t. 24
u. 25
v. 26
w. 27
x. 28
y. 29
z. 30

20-16-9-5-23-9
27-5-16-15
29-19-29-19
17-19-17

Irene and Noah decoded the note.

Noah asked, "Who's Yo-yo?"

Irene replied, "My dog."

This is the note from Irene's mom. Can you decode it?

18

Irene wrote the letters *a-z* down the side of a notebook page. Then she wrote numbers under the letters. Irene said, "On Monday, the number 1 stands for the letter *a*. On Tuesday, the second day, 2 stands for *a*. Friday is the fifth day, so 5 stands for *a*."

Decode It

"I get it," said Noah. "So in Friday's plus 5 code, *a* is 5, *b* is 6, *c* is 7, *d* is 8, *e* is 9, and *f* equals 10."

"That's the idea!" said Irene. "All the way to 30 for *z*."

19

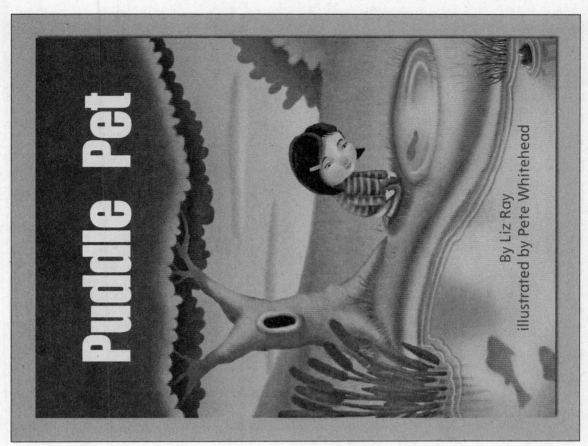

Puddle Pet

By Liz Ray

illustrated by Pete Whitehead

Puddle Pet

"Look at my new pet," said Jen.
"I found it in a big puddle."
Her friends huddled near Jen's
bowl. A small dark speck swam
over some pebbles.
"It's only a fish," grumbled Jake.
"A fish is nothing special."

22

© Macmillan/McGraw-Hill

"I think this fish is special,"
Jen told the group. "I'll name him
Speckle." She jiggled the bowl and
light sparkled off the fish.

"You can't play with a fish or
cuddle it," said Jake.

"I like to watch him," said Jen.

23

"See what Speckle can do now,"
Jen called to her friends.

"A fish can only blow bubbles
and swim," said Jake.

"But Speckle isn't a fish," Jen
said, putting her pet on the table.

"He's a frog, and he can jump!"

26

275

Jen took good care of Speckle. She fed him and cleaned his bowl each day. It was fun to watch Speckle swim and blow bubbles.

One day, Jen saw that her fish had little back legs. She was puzzled. Fish don't have legs! What was going on?

24

Jen kept watching her pet. As Speckle got bigger, his legs got bigger too. Then he grew front legs. His tail became shorter and his body changed shape.

Jen had learned something important. Speckle was not a fish!

25

Doggy Door

Doggy Door

by Liane B. Onish

illustrated by Erin Mauterer

The basement door was open. Mom said, "Cody, didn't I remind you to close the basement door last night?"

"I did remember, Mom. But she opened it," Cody said.

"Where is she?" Mom asked.

Doggy Door

There she was. Sophie, the Irish sheepdog, was sound asleep on the new sofa.

Mom said, "In order to keep the new sofa looking new, Sophie needs to sleep in the basement. How did she get out?"

Doggy Door

29

After Cody returned from taking Sophie for a walk, the basement door was open.

"What are you doing, Mom?" he asked.

"I am putting in a new lock!" she said.

32

30

"Sophie opened the door herself," Cody said.

"I don't believe it! Show me!" Mom said.

So Cody, Mom, and Sophie went into the basement and closed the door.

Doggy Door

Sophie stood on the third step and jumped up. Her big front paws hit the doorknob and slid off. Sophie repeated the jumping and pawing until the doorknob turned.

31

The
Camping Trip

by Liz Ray

illustrated by Cheryl Mendenhall

The Camping Trip

Dad took Max and Jill camping in a local desert for several days.

"I don't like it here," Max grumbled. "It's too hot and dry."

"I can't see a single living thing," said Jill. "Just rocks, pebbles, and sand blowing in the wind."

2

The Camping Trip

Dad made a simple supper of hot dogs, pickles, and apples. They ate by the light of a candle. Then Max and Jill crawled into their sleeping bags.

In the middle of the night, a strange sound filled the tent.

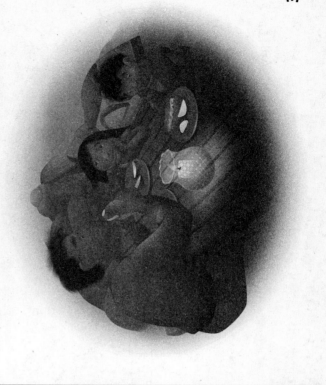

3

Max saw a lizard scramble up a rock. A hawk soared over them.

That night they watched the stars twinkle and sparkle like a shiny nickel. A soft wind ruffled their hair.

"I like the desert now," said Max.

"So do I," said Jill.

6

"Listen!" said Jill. She trembled.

"It sounds like a howling giggle!"

"What is it?" Max asked, huddled in his sleeping bag.

"I think it's a coyote," said Dad. "They live in the desert."

4

The Camping Trip

The next day, the kids and Dad went on a hike.

"Look at these marks in the sand," said Dad. "I think snakes made them."

"These look like mouse footprints," said Jill.

5

The Turtle

by Liz Ray

illustrated by Jeremy Tugeau

One weekend, Kaylin followed a footpath to the pond. She sat under a willow tree. This was the area she loved best.

Kaylin looked down and saw a turtle under some roots. It seemed very feeble.

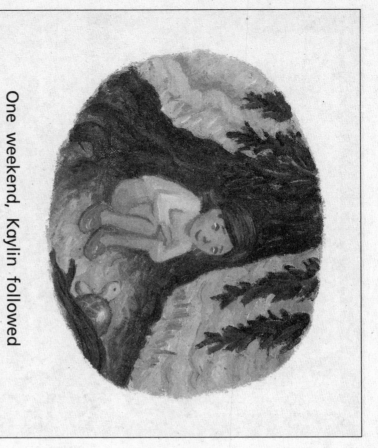

8

The Turtle

"Poor fellow," said Kaylin. "I'll take care of you." She took the turtle home and put it in a yellow box. She gave the turtle a shallow pan of water and a leaf. But the turtle remained very still.

9

First the turtle ate a piece of a daisy. Then it crawled into the shallow water and ate a minnow. When Kaylin stood, her shadow fell over the turtle. It hid in its shell until she moved.

"You will be fine," she said. "You can take care of yourself."

12

287

10

Kaylin got some money and went to the bookstore. She bought a booklet about turtles. The booklet explained that turtles rest all winter. They wake up in spring. It also said that turtles should remain in the wild.

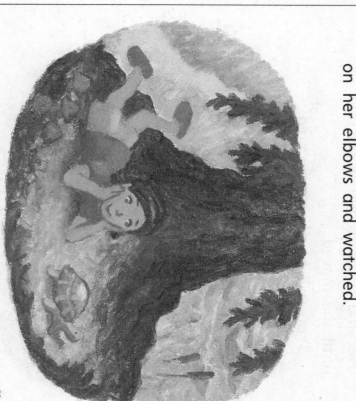

The Turtle

"It's spring now," said Kaylin. "I'll return my turtle to the pond." Kaylin took the turtle back to the pond. She put the turtle next to some flowers. Then she leaned on her elbows and watched.

11

288

Tadpole Decides

by Liane B. Onish
illustrated by Richard Bernal

Tadpole swam beside the reeds next to Fish. Tadpole decided he was a fish. "Hello, Fish," said Tadpole. "Look, I am a fish, too."

"Are you sure?" asked Fish.

Tadpole said, "I have a tail like a fish. But a fish is round and I am skinny."

14

Tadpole Decides

Snake slithered by. Tadpole decided he was a snake. "Hi, Snake," said Tadpole. "Look, I am a snake, too."

"Are you sure?" asked Snake. Tadpole said, "I am thin like a snake. But a snake is long and I am short." Tadpole was not so sure.

15

Tadpole Decides

The next morning, he leaped out of the water. "I am not a fish, a snake, or a turtle!" he said.

"And you are not a tadpole!" said Frog, sitting alone on the grass.

"Look, I am a frog, too," said the grown-up tadpole. "And I am sure."

18

Soon, Tadpole began to change. His whole body was not skinny like Snake's. Tadpole had four legs and a tail. He was so excited! Tadpole saw Turtle. Tadpole decided he was now a turtle.

16

© Macmillan/McGraw-Hill

"Hello, Turtle," said Tadpole.

"Look, I am a turtle, too."

"Are you sure?" asked Turtle as she drew her legs and tail inside her shell. Tadpole did not have a shell.

"I am not sure," he said sadly.

17

The Rainy Day

by Liz Ray

illustrated by Melanie Siegel

The Rainy Day

It was the biggest rainstorm of the year. Sam had remained inside all weekend. Now he leaned on his elbows and watched raindrops slide down the window.

"I'm bored," Sam complained.

"Can I go outside?"

The Rainy Day

"Put on your raincoat and boots," said Mom. "And don't get near the river."

Sam followed a footpath up the hill. He saw lots of footprints in the mud. A tall girl stood at the top of the hill. She looked down at the river.

The Rainy Day

Just then Sam and the girl saw a man in a rowboat. He helped the man in the yellow coat into the boat. The man was safe at last! Sam was glad. And he was not bored anymore either!

24

22

Sam saw a man in a yellow raincoat standing on the footbridge. "He must measure how high the river gets," explained the girl. "We need to know if it will flood." Sam had lots of questions but he had no time to ask them.

The Rainy Day

As he watched the man complete his task, Sam saw a log rush downstream.

It crashed into the footbridge and knocked the man into the river. He struggled to grab a willow branch, but the water was not shallow enough to stand in. "He needs help!" yelled the girl.

23

How Bird Was Lured Away from Fire

by Emma Searle
illustrated by Kim Howard

How Bird Was Lured Away from Fire

26

This story is a retelling of an old, old tale about fire. The tale tells how a man got fire by luring it away from a bird.

Bird was an odd creature. She had wings like other birds, but she could not fly. So she walked around the grasslands and the towns, looking for food and drink.

How Bird Was Lured Away from Fire

One day Bird found Fire on the ground. She hid Fire under her wing, hoping to keep it all to herself.

Soon Bird grew tired and thirsty. So she went into a building to get a water bottle out of a machine.

Bird went back outside to drink her water, but she couldn't open the bottle.

How Bird Was Lured Away from Fire

27

30

Bird pretended not to care about the dream. But the next day, she stood on a hill. She put Fire on the ground. Then she stretched out her wings and waited. Just then the man snatched Fire and ran away. The man was very happy again. Now he could use Fire to help people of all cultures. He was sure that he could show them how to use Fire in many safe ways.

Just then a scientist who worked in the building stepped outside. He saw Bird struggling with her bottle. When she raised her wings, the man saw Fire.

"Bird has Fire," he thought. "Surely, that is mine! I must get it back from Bird!"

The man thought and thought about how to lure Bird away from Fire. At last he had an idea.

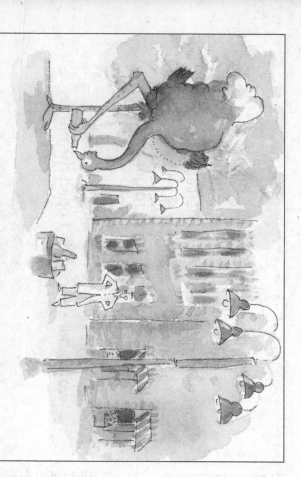

28

© Macmillan/McGraw-Hill

The man went up to Bird. "Bird, we must talk. I saw into the future last night. I dreamed you were flying!"

This upset Bird because she could not fly. But she stayed to hear more.

"You stood high on a hill with your wings completely stretched out. A gust of wind lifted you up. You were flying!" said the man. "And there was no wire!"

29

Name_____

School and Classroom

I go to _____ School.

My teacher is _____ .

What grade are you in?
I am in second grade.

Tips

- Practice with a partner or your teacher.

- Use words you know.

- Try out a new word.

Is this your classroom?
Yes, it is.

Come in and sit down.
Thank you.

Ask for Information: Pretend it's the first day of school. You want to find the cafeteria. Who would you ask? What would you say? Practice asking for information with a partner. Take turns asking questions.

To the Teacher: Tell students that they will practice communicating using formal language. Explain that when speaking to a teacher or classmates, they should speak in complete sentences and use words like please and thank you. Model how to say each sentence and have them repeat after you. Then have them role-play with a partner. Have children play online **Newcomer Game 1:** Introduce Self.

Grade 2 Unit 1   301

Classroom Commands

1. Sit down at your desks.

2. Stand up, please.

3. Line up at the door.

4. Write your name neatly.

5. Open your books.

6. Close your books.

7. Trade papers.

8. Pack up your things.

Tips

- Practice speaking with a partner.

- Use movements to help you explain.

- Try out new words.

To the Teacher: Tell children that they will practice listening to and following classroom commands. Give each command and model how to follow it. Have children repeat the command and the action. Then have children take turns giving commands to their classmates. Have them play online **Newcomer Game 5:** Commands and Imperatives.

Name_____

Food

I like _____ and _____ .

I'm hungry.
May I please have a snack?
I like crackers and cheese.

I'm thirsty.
May I please have a drink?
I like milk and juice.

Thank you!

Tips

- Take turns speaking and listening.

- Use gestures to help explain.

- Use pictures or real items to show what a word means.

Ask for Information: Pretend you are in a grocery store. You want to find the milk. What do you say? How do you ask? Practice asking for information with a partner. Take turns asking questions.

To the Teacher: Tell children that they will practice communicating using formal language. Explain that when speaking to a teacher or classmate, they should speak in complete sentences and use works like "May I" and "thank you" when making requests. Model how to say each sentence and have them repeat after you. Have children role play with a partner and then play online **Newcomer Game 2:** Basic Requests.

School Helpers

Many people work at our school.

The _____ works at our school.

Please meet our principal.
How are you today?

This is your bus driver.
Good morning!

Tips

- Repeat words you hear.

- Listen to others when they speak.

- Practice with a partner.

Say hello to the school nurse.
Hello. It's nice to meet you.

Our custodian cleans the classroom.
Thank you!

To the Teacher: Tell children that they will practice communicating using formal language. Explain that when asking a question they should use more formal language, especially when speaking to an adult or someone they do not know well. Model how to say questions and have children repeat after you. Have children role play with a partner and then play online **Newcomer Game 4:** Some People and Places.

Classroom Routines

Look at the clock.

Look at the calendar.

Is it time for lunch?

We do math in the morning.

Tips

- Practice speaking with a partner.

- Use the clock to help you tell the time.

- Use the calendar to help you name the day.

Ask for Information: Practice asking for information with a partner. Take turns asking questions.

What day is it? It's _____.

What time is it? It's time for _____.

To the Teacher: Tell children that they will be learning and using routine language needed for classroom communications. Have children practice giving classroom directions using formal language. They should use phrases such as, "please," and "May I." Sometimes words like please and thank you are not used. Model and have them repeat after you. Then have children role play with a partner and then play online **Newcomer Game 15:** Question Words.

Grade 2 Unit 5 (305)

Name _____

Health and Feelings

1. May I please go to the nurse's office?

2. I don't feel well.

3. I have a headache.

4. My leg hurts.

5. I need help.

Tips

- Practice speaking with a partner.

- Use gestures to show what you mean.

- Ask for help when you need it.

Ask for Information: Practice asking for information with a partner. Take turns asking questions.

Can you help me _____?

Will you show me _____?

Take turns practicing with a partner.

To the Teacher: Tell children that they will practice telling their teacher or the school nurse how they feel. Demonstrate to confirm meaning. Model saying each sentence and have children repeat after you. Remind them to use gestures as they speak. Then have them draw pictures and role play the sentences with a partner.

Name _____

Practice reading the words you know. Work with a partner.

a	always	yellow	pull	best
even	would	year	the	shout
nothing	hold	cold	long	under
begin	your	run	of	America
go	because	minutes	to	world
study	across	pick	can	friends
six	off	English	are	understand
blue	language	move	house	drink
from	orange	instead	do	give
another	picture	country	write	work

Find the words your teacher says aloud. Circle the words.

Beginning/Intermediate Have partners read all the words they know to one another. Then read aloud the high-frequency words for the week. Have partners locate each weekly word and circle it. Return to this page each week. Monitor as partners read the newly acquired sight vocabulary with increasing accuracy.

Name _____

Practice reading the words you know. Work with a partner.

special	morning	other	my	ten
like	different	anything	scientist	our
over	buy	school	grew	found
does	funny	call	her	there
though	small	about	girl	way
up	now	out	building	they
don't	never	before	who	been
island	against	for	should	fast
eat	straight	began	machine	said
word	number	everyone	myself	come

Find the words your teacher says aloud. Circle the words.

© Macmillan/McGraw-Hill

Beginning/Intermediate Have partners read all the words they know to one another. Then read aloud the high-frequency words for the week. Have partners locate each weekly word and circle it. Return to this page each week. Monitor as partners read the newly acquired sight vocabulary with increasing accuracy.

Name _____

Practice reading the words you know. Work with a partner.

five	these	body	behind	we
after	believe	full	one	boy
tell	first	heavy	happened	this
new	be	young	those	were
mother	their	much	what	better
away	both	which	ball	system
you	built	find	old	carry
two	material	no	pretty	once
fall	then	start	father	around
could	not	inside	talk	region

Find the words your teacher says aloud. Circle the words.

Beginning/Intermediate Have partners read all the words they know to one another. Then read aloud the high-frequency words for the week. Have partners locate each weekly word and circle it. Return to this page each week. Monitor as partners read the newly acquired sight vocabulary with increasing accuracy.

Practice reading the words you know. Work with a partner.

family	ride	color	open	paper
bring	early	enough	gave	air
place	little	wish	and	along
all	where	eight	among	eyes
hear	thought	poor	wash	with
or	three	follow	decided	city
four	play	song	read	sound
today	any	also	sleep	far
water	again	people	bought	below
above	some	near	why	own

Find the words your teacher says aloud. Circle the words.

Beginning/Intermediate Have partners read all the words they know to one another. Then read aloud the high-frequency words for the week. Have partners locate each weekly word and circle it. Return to this page each week. Monitor as partners read the newly acquired sight vocabulary with increasing accuracy.

Name _____

Practice reading the words you know. Work with a partner.

use	put	how	draw	knew
by	food	certain	idea	group
I	together	right	second	only
door	too	walked	learn	want
remember	more	many	until	hurt
order	soon	know	into	laugh
seven	so	gone	build	very
climbed	every	upon	good	searching
got	through	field	often	change
light	clean	important	hundred	goes

Find the words your teacher says aloud. Circle the words.

© Macmillan/McGraw-Hill

Beginning/Intermediate Have partners read all the words they know to one another. Then read aloud the high-frequency words for the week. Have partners locate each weekly word and circle it. Return to this page each week. Monitor as partners read the newly acquired sight vocabulary with increasing accuracy.

Grade 2 Unit 5   311

Name _____

Practice reading the words you know. Work with a partner.

is	done	green	it	show
jump	live	cut	sit	has
listen	during	area	brought	pulled
see	made	kind	shall	grow
me	look	complete	was	help
wind	whole	love	questions	voice
says	great	make	he	piece
saw	down	try	keep	she
several	sure	money	measure	travel
have	here	warm	head	sing

Find the words your teacher says aloud. Circle the words.

Beginning/Intermediate Have partners read all the words they know to one another. Then read aloud the high-frequency words for the week. Have partners locate each weekly word and circle it. Return to this page each week. Monitor as partners read the newly acquired sight vocabulary with increasing accuracy.